Europe 2000: What kind of television?

The European Cultural Foundation

The European Cultural Foundation (Amsterdam) is a private, non-profit-making independent body, the aims of which are to promote European cultural cooperation. "European" denotes both Western and Eastern Europe. "Culture" refers not only to Europe's past and present artistic richness, but includes the various sectors of European Society: education, the environment, social policy and the media. The Foundation was established in Geneva in 1954 by Denis de Rougemont, Hendrik Brugmans and Robert Schuman and moved to Amsterdam in 1960. To achieve its objectives, the Foundation operates a grants programme to provide support for European projects and a network of Research Institutes and Centres which engage in comparative research in various fields from a European perspective. Since 1960, the Foundation has an official agreement of cooperation with the Council of Europe and in the 80s it is managing the European Community exchange and information programmes in education, *Eurydice* and *Erasmus*. *The European Institute for the Media*, created in 1983, is part of the Foundation's network.

The European Institute for the Media

The Institute is the European centre for policy-oriented research and development in the fields of radio, television, the press and related issues in mass communications.

It was founded in 1983 by the European Cultural Foundation in co-operation with the University of Manchester. The activities of the Institute include research and development projects bearing on public policy in Europe; the maintenance of the Documentation Centre on European Media, conferences and seminars for policy makers and the training of media specialists.

The Institute publishes the results of its research in the Media Monograph series, and issues the quarterly *Media Bulletin* containing current information about media policy developments in Europe.

THE EUROPEAN CULTURAL FOUNDATION
THE EUROPEAN INSTITUTE FOR THE MEDIA

Europe 2000:
What kind of television?

Report of the
European Television Task Force

President Valéry Giscard d'Estaing

June 1988

With a translation of the Summary and
Recommendations into German and Dutch

© 1988 The European Institute for the Media,
The University , Manchester, M13 9PL
United Kingdom

ISBN 0948195 17 7

The cover design is taken from the mural *Links*, by Leda Luss, in the entrance hall of the European Institute for the Media in Manchester

Foreword
by the President of the European
Television Task Force

Europe is witnessing spectacular developments in the most pervasive of its means of mass communication: television. Three converging phenomena, the development of new communications technologies, the deregulation of control arrangements and the internationalisation of structures, are playing their parts in changing both the traditional ways of organising television and the habits of the consumers. A movement has begun which will cause significant changes in the televisual landscape of Europe.

Television in Europe developed essentially within national frameworks. For technical, economic, political and cultural reasons the organisation of television was structured to serve the interests of each individual country. The growth of television in response to national needs was reinforced by the linguistic diversity of Europe. To think of television in the context of European interdependence therefore demands a modification of the national broadcasting policies which have, for over a generation, held sway in most European countries. At present the old order is breaking up without any clear indication of the form which the new order will take.

Our brief

In this situation the European Cultural Foundation and the European Institute for the Media decided to appoint a Task Force to explore the new order. In the Spring of 1987, they invited a group of experienced men and women from a representative group of European countries to "consider and report upon the future structure and content of television receivable in more than one country in Europe by terrestrial transmission, satellite and cable, both by services originating there and by services receivable from elsewhere."[1]

---

1   The full text of the Terms of Reference is given on Page viii

---

The Task Force was given a year to achieve its task, being asked to report to the Governors of the Foundation and the Council of the Institute in June 1988. I am glad to say that we have fulfilled that mandate.

Membership

Given the politically, nationally and economically sensitive character of television, the composition of the Task Force was an achievement in itself. The membership included a balanced group of politicians from the mainstream of European politics. Thirteen of the Member States of the Council of Europe and nine of the Member States of the European Community were represented among the members of the Task Force. Their origins ranged from Portugal to Sweden and from Italy to Norway. The fact that this broad range of countries with their distinctive traditions will probably be exposed to the same satellite signals illustrates the issues which the Task Force had to face. There was also a representative group of television professionals from the public and the private sectors, as well as producers, media researchers and experts in information technology.

In view of the delicate nature of so many of the issues affecting television, the independence of the Task Force has been an asset. Appointed by two bodies concerned first and last with the welfare of the people of Europe, the Task Force was able to go to work without institutional constraints. It invited observers from the Commission of the European Communities and the Council of Europe, without being limited by the terms of reference of either. It preferred to work under sometimes spartan conditions rather than to be beholden to major financial benefactors.

Methods of Work

The Task Force has held seven plenary meetings as well as meetings of its Steering and Drafting Committees and of two Working Groups, on the structural matters and programme policy respectively. The Task Force took oral evidence in Belgium, Denmark, France, Ireland, the Federal Republic of Germany, Finland, Italy, the Netherlands, Norway, Portugal, Spain, Sweden and the United Kingdom. We also heard evidence from the Commission of the European Communities and from the Council of Europe. An observer appointed by the European Broadcasting Union ensured that the point of view of the Union was represented. Evidence was also submitted by a large number of other organisations and institutions[1]

The Issues

Our report falls into two parts. Part A asks why television matters. Chapter 1 considers the rôle that television plays in the lives of the citizens of Europe. Chapter 2 looks at the changes in the television landscape caused by broadcast technology, changing socio-economic structures and the attitudes of viewers. Chapter 3 addresses the difficult issue of quality in television: how it can be defined and the extent to which financial resources and quality are related.

Part B of the Report considers possible action to promote the best in European television. At a time when technological and economic developments tend to concentrate on the supply side of television there is a risk of underestimating the elasticity of demand. Chapter 4 assesses the effort being made to develop a framework for competition Europe, mainly by statutory means, in the European Community and the Council of Europe. In Chapter 5 we identify the urgent need to develop a more dynamic film and television industry in Europe so as to provide more good quality programmes for the expanding number of services. In each case the Task Force has found itself in agreement on a wide range of positive recommendations.

In Chapter 6 we describe the range of transfrontier television services. This expansion arises mainly in the private sector and from the need which some public television services feel to undertake their own development in the international field. The Task Force also considered the lessons to be drawn from the closure of the **Europa tv** service. We do not think that this should be regarded as invalidating the concept of European television services in the public interest and we propose some alternative models for the realisation of this concept.

The Task Force found, in the course of its visits, that the main concern expressed in European countries is about the consequences of the segmentation of the audiences for national television services. We found also that the new transfrontier television services have begun to operate on assumptions quite different from those of the established public service channels. Instead of seeking a substantial audience in one country, transfrontier channels are content with only a small percentage of the aggregate audience across Europe.

1   A complete list of those submitting evidence is contained in Annex 1

We also discovered a tendency towards the development of a two-tier economy in television. The existing national public service organisations base their programming on substantial programme budgets, averaging between 50 000 ecu and 100 000 ecu per hour. This provides adequate scope for programme origination and production. The programme budgets of new commercial entrepreneurs, on the other hand appear to amount to only 2 000 ecu and 5 000 ecu per hour, making them wholly dependent on cheap imported mass-produced programmes. For round- the-clock transmission these companies rely heavily on multiple repeats.

A European Television Forum

Diverse as is the membership of the Task Force, we were able to agree the substantial number of important recommendations listed in Chapter 8. The ones most likely to shape the future of television in Europe are the proposals to establish a European Television Forum. The maintenance and development of good television in Europe requires more than the basic statutory provisions proposed by the European Community and the Council of Europe. Television is too important in the lives of the people of Europe to be left entirely to the market place. The proposed European Television Forum (Chapter 7) will have a number of rôles: to promote good practice among the public and private broadcasters; to encourage competition in quality among the programme producers; to facilitate the exchange of views between programme providers and television viewers; to monitor the quality and quantity of advertising on television; to help with language transfer so as to ease programme flow between European countries; to develop among television personnel an understanding of their common European vocation; and to encourage well-informed discussion of the evolution of television in Europe. We leave open the possible development of the forum into a body to which national governments or the European institutions might, in the interests of Europe as a whole, assign certain functions in relation to cross-frontier broadcasting. We are confident that the Forum we propose will develop a momentum of its own and will come to exercise a beneficial and creative influence on European television in the years to come.

Paris, May 1988

Valéry Giscard d'Estaing

Acknowledgements

The Task Force is indebted to the many people who have contributed to this Report. The European Institute for the Media which provided the Secretariat, Staff and Advisers has in particular borne the main burden of the organisation of hearings and meetings, the sifting of material, and the writing and the editing of the report. Other experts who have contributed in their respective fields include M. Bernard Blin, Chef du département des affaires internationales, SJTI du Premier Ministre (France), M. Pierre Desgraupes, President of SOFICA Créations and Chairman of the Advisory Council of the European Institute for the Media (France), Dr Helmut Drück, Head of the Planning Department Television, Westdeutscher Rundfunk (FRG), Mr Klaas Jan Hindriks, NOB (Netherlands), Mr Wolfgang Lehr, former Director-General of Hessischer Rundfunk (FRG), Mr Charles Levison, Managing Director, Virgin Satellite Operations (UK), Mr Jeremy Mitchell, Chairman of the Communications sub-committee of OICU (UK), Mr Richard Schoonhoven, Director of Katholieke Radio Omroep (Netherlands) and Dr Karl Günther von Hase, first Chairman of the European Institute for the Media and former Director General of ZDF (FRG).

The Task Force also acknowledges the support which enabled it to carry out its task. The financial support of the European Cultural Foundation and the infrastructure provided by the European Institute for the Media created the conditions without which it could not have done its work. Additional support in cash and kind was contributed by Antenne 2 (France), ARD (FRG), BRT (Belgische Radio en Televisie, Belgium), the Council of Europe, the European Cinema and Television Year 1988, FR3 (France), the Independent Broadcasting Authority (United Kingdom), NOS/NOB (Netherlands), NRK (Norsk Rikskringkasting, Norway), RAI Radiotelevisione Italiana, (Italy), RTBF (Radio-Télévision Belge de la Communauté Française, Belgium), Sky Channel (United Kingdom), Swiss Broadcasting Corporation, (Switzerland), Thames Television (UK) and TF1 (France). To all these organisations the Task Force expresses its appreciation.

Terms of Reference of the European Television Task Force

The terms of reference established by the European Cultural Foundation and the European Institute for the Media in April 1987:

"Taking account of the terms of the Declaration of the Board of Governors of the European Cultural Foundation adopted on 30th May 1986, *Towards a Coherent Media Policy in Europe*[1], of the proposals of the EC Commission, of the conclusions of the meeting of Ministers responsible for Communications held by the Council of Europe in December 1986, and other relevant activities in this field,

The aims of the European Television Task Force are as follows:

to consider and report upon the future structure and content of television receivable in more than one country in Europe by terrestrial transmission, satellite and cable, both by services originating in Europe and those originating elsewhere:

And in particular to consider and report upon

(a) whether programme quality can and should be secured in the services which will be available to European audiences;
(b) how such quality could be secured, whether by regulation at the European level and/or by other means;
(c) the scope for co-operatively operated public services for Europe;
(d) the impact of the use of video tapes on television viewing;
(e) the impact of international transmissions on national services."[2]

1   See Annex 3
2   The European Cultural Foundation and the European Institute for the Media, document no. EIM/P/055, Manchester and Amsterdam, 4 September 1986

The European Television Task Force
1987 — 1988

Valéry Giscard d'Estaing President	*President of the Republic of France 1974-1981; Chairman of the Foreign Affairs Committee of the National Assembly.*	**France**
Giorgio la Malfa Chairman	*National Secretary of the Republican Party of Italy; Professor of Economics in the University of Turin.*	**Italy**
Francisco Pinto Balsemão Co-Chairman	*Prime Minister of Portugal 1981-1983; Chairman Sojomal. S.a.r.l.*	**Portugal**
Michèle Cotta Co-Chairman	*Director of Information of TF1; Chairman of the Haute autorité de la communication audiovisuelle 1981-1986.*	**France**
Javier Baviano Corresponding member	*Director General of PRISA.*	**Spain**
Antoine de Clermont-Tonnerre	*President of Editions mondiales; Member of the Board of Directors of TF1.*	**France**
Jürgen Doetz	*Managing Director of SAT-1.*	**Federal Republic of Germany**

Massimo Fichera	*Deputy-Director (Planning) of RAI Radiotelevisione Italiana.*	**Italy**
John Gau	*Managing Director John Gau Productions; Chairman of the Royal Television Society.*	**United Kingdom**
Raymond Georis	*Secretary General of the European Cultural Foundation, Amsterdam.*	**Belgium**
Bjartmar Gjerde Corresponding member	*Director General of Norskrikskringkasting (NRK).*	**Norway**
Joan Majó Cruzate Chairman of the Drafting Committee	*Chairman of Olivetti S.A. (Spain); Minister for Industry and Electronics 1985 - 1986.*	**Spain**
Peter Radel	*Administrative Director of Oesterreichischer Rundfunk (ORF).*	**Austria**
Antonio Riva	*Director General of the Swiss Broadcasting Corporation.*	**Switzerland**
Peter Schiwy	*Director General of Norddeutscher Rundfunk (NDR).*	**Federal Republic of Germany**
Gaston Thorn	*Chairman of the Compagnie Luxembourgeoise de Télédiffusion (CLT); President of the Commission of the European Communities 1981 - 1985.*	**Luxemburg**

Sir Ian Trethowan	*Chairman of Thames Television; Director General of the British Broadcasting Corporation (BBC) 1977-1982.*	**United Kingdom**
Adriaan Verhulst	*Chairman of the Board, Belgische Radio en Televisie (BRT)(1969-1980 and 1984-1988); Professor of Mediæval History in the Universities of Ghent and Brussels.*	**Belgium**
Gijs de Vries	*Member of the European Parliament.*	**Netherlands**
Anne-Margrete Wachtmeister	*Media Consultant at Sveriges Radio, 1968-1975, 1980-1986.*	**Sweden**
George Wedell	*Director of the European Institute for the Media; Professor of Communications Policy in the University of Manchester.*	**United Kingdom**

Advisers

| **Rudolf Gressmann** | *Visiting Fellow of the European Institute for the Media; Director of the EBU Technical Centre 1974-1986.* | **Federal Republic of Germany** |
| **Anthony Pragnell** | *Visiting Fellow of the European Institute for the Media; Member of the Board of Directors of Channel Four Television; Deputy Director General of the Independent Broadcasting Authority (IBA) 1961-1983.* | **United Kingdom** |

Robert Wangermée	*Vice-Chairman of the European Institute for the Media; Vice-Chairman of TV5; Vice-président du Conseil supérieur de l'audiovisuel de la Communauté française de Belgique.*	**Belgium**

Observers

Peter Leuprecht	*Director of Human Rights, Council of Europe.*	**Austria**
Mariano Maggiore	*Head of Division, Directorate for Information, Communication and Culture (DG X) of the Commission of the European Communities.*	**Italy**
Miro Vilcek	*Head of the Television programme Division of the European Broadcasting Union.*	**Yugoslavia**

Secretariat

Georg-Michael Luyken Executive Secretary	*Deputy Director of the European Institute for the Media.*	**Federal Republic of Germany**
Philip Crookes	*Assistant Director (Programmes) of the European Institute for the Media.*	**United Kingdom**
Janneke Geene	*Editorial Assistant in the European Institute for the Media.*	**Netherlands**
Mario Hirsch	*Secretary of the Parti démocratique of Luxemburg.*	**Luxemburg**

André Lange	*Attaché in the Directorate of Human Rights, Council of Europe. Visiting Fellow of the European Institute for the Media.*	**Belgium**
Jean-Luc Renaud	*Leverhulme Stipendiary Fellow of the European Institute for the Media.*	**Switzerland**
Jo Travis	*Project Assistant in the European Institute for the Media.*	**United Kingdom**

Abbreviations and currencies

Throughout this Report we have used the ISO standard abbreviations for the names of countries where they appear in lists and tables, and have based the alphabetical ordering of our tables on these abbreviations. Comparisons of money sums have been made in European currency units, **ecu**. The following list shows the ISO standard abbreviation for each country and the exchange rate used as a basis of calculation for conversion from that country's national currency into ecu.

ISO abbreviation and Country		Currency	1 ecu =
A	Austria	Schilling	14.60
B	Belgium	Belgian franc	43.42
CH	Switzerland	Swiss franc	1.72
D	Federal Republic of Germany	Deutschmark	2.08
DK	Denmark	Kroner	7.98
E	Spain	Peseta	137.12
F	France	French franc	7.04
GB	United Kingdom	Pound sterling	0.66
GR	Greece	Drachma	166.43
I	Italy	Lira	1543.06
IRL	Ireland	Punt	0.78
L	Luxemburg	Luxemburg franc	43.42
N	Norway	Kroner	7.63
NL	Netherlands	Guilder	2.33
P	Portugal	Escudo	168.30
S	Sweden	Kronor	7.28
SF	Finland	Markka	4.90
USA	United States of America	Dollar	1.23

Contents

Part A

Chapter 1: Television in the Lives of the People   1

Chapter 2: The New European Audiovisual Landscape   13

Part B

List of Tables

Chapter 1
Television in the lives of the people

The uses of television

In most countries of the world, in less than forty years, television has come to play a major role in people's lives. In Europe as in every industrialised part of the globe, it has taken its place in almost every home. Television requires the more or less active attention of many people for two or three hours a day on average, and this period may be even longer when some channels transmit programmes almost around the clock (see Table 1.1). Television viewing is mainly a leisure activity. A useful criterion of the importance of television is the proportion of the individual's disposable leisure time which it absorbs. Thus the 2-3 hours of viewing a day has to be seen in the context of a normal day consisting of 7-8 hours of work, 7-8 hours of sleep as well as 1-2 hours of travel to and from work and between 1 and 3 hours at meals (which may of course be eaten in front of the television). These activities leave 4 to 5 hours of disposable time per day for leisure, of which more than half is, on average, spent before the television screen. In quantitative terms this makes television by far the most substantial activity during the disposable time of the individual. For many people television provides their principal means of relaxation after a hard day's work; this is its positive contribution to the current European life-style. But just because this is so, we consider that television needs to recognise its important role in activating viewers to thought, reaction and reflection, in stimulating their interest in the world around them and in encouraging them to take responsible decisions about their own lives.

If television is so powerful, it is because it allows those who watch it to take advantage of it in a number of ways, depending on their education, their tastes and their psycho-cultural needs. Viewers tend to use television first and foremost for entertainment or escapism, whether through imaginative drama or through variety and game-shows. But television has the capacity to do far more: it can offer viewers the chance to be informed, to gain vicarious experience of the external world, to learn, and to cultivate their minds. This powerful hold which television has over the lives and minds of people is a justification for the reflections which the European Television Task Force has attempted to bring to bear on the important changes which the television industry is now experiencing.

Until very recently, television developed within a strict national framework. As there were few frequencies which could be used by terrestrial transmitters, so that only limited numbers of services were available in the area which they covered, the first task of national governments was to share out the frequencies, to grant broadcasting concessions and to determine how the various services were to be financed.

In Europe, the frequencies were usually reserved for public corporations which enjoyed a monopoly or shared an oligopoly of two or three, and which received the income from licences and subventions, in some cases deriving additional income from advertising revenues. In return these public services were expected by law, by regulation or by convention to provide a public service of information, education and culture as well as entertainment.

In the United States, frequencies were generally allocated to private enterprises deriving their income from advertising. The majority of these stations are affiliated to one or other of the three major networks: ABC, CBS and NBC, while a fourth network, Fox Broadcasting, is currently establishing itself. This apparently liberal system has grown up within the constraints of an organisational and regulatory framework under the control of the Federal Communications Commission, which allocates channels, grants or suspends permission to broadcast, fixes technical standards and lays down a number of cultural and ethical aims for programmes. The fact that finance comes exclusively from advertising has meant that the programmes shown by the American networks are mainly designed for entertainment, but must conform to FCC regulations governing their content and moral standards. The FCC can invoke sanctions ranging from warning notices, through cash penalties to suspension or withdrawal of the broadcasting licence against a broadcaster found to be in breach of the prescribed regulations.

During the last twenty years, first in North America and then in Europe, the system by which television was traditionally organised has been challenged, as has the long-established dominance of the major networks in the United States and the national public services in Europe.

This challenge has been made possible by such technical developments as:

Table 1.1: Average daily viewing in 1985, and increase to 1988 for the four largest markets

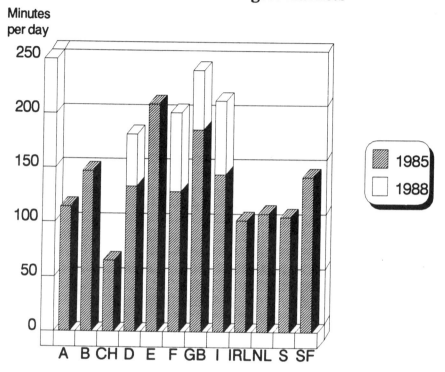

Source: E.G. Wedell & G-M. Luyken, "Media In Competition"
European Institute for the Media/ InterMedia Congress Hamburg, Manchester & Hamburg 1986,
"Eurodience",Paris, 8/1988: Page 2.

- **cable**, which by greatly increasing the number of channels in a specific area, puts an end to the excuse that few frequencies are available;

- **satellites**, which ensure that the programmes which they carry are transmitted over the whole continent and override national boundaries; they can be *fixed-service satellites*, the signals from which are received by large collective aerials and carried to viewers through the cable networks; or *direct-broadcast satellites*, the signals from which are received by individual aerials;

- **video**, which turns programmes of every kind (and especially films) into commodities which can be marketed in the same way as books and records and allows them to circulate by being bought or hired.

Proliferation of services and public accountability

The proliferation of broadcasting and the greatly increased range of programmes made possible by cable, satellite and video may create new needs. An optimistic point of view which is often expressed nowadays in Europe and in the United States is that these numerous channels may fundamentally transform communication. By specialising, each of them will be able to cater for the needs, tastes and interests of the widely differing groups to be found within a society which is finally ceasing to be a mass audience. Hence, there could be such services as entertainment channels offering non-stop cinema, music channels catering to the tastes of people of different ages, educational channels, cultural channels for lovers of opera, concerts or the theatre, and channels for linguistic and ethnic minorities.

This proliferation of television services is modelled on the press, in which general newspapers coexist with regional or local ones, and with specialised magazines. It is true that technological developments make it possible for television to move from the level of mass communication to that of group communication. But the perfect balance between demand and supply is even more theoretical in television than in the case of the press.

In the last few years, television has been considered in North America as a particularly promising area of profit. For this reason, the traditional terrestrial television stations, especially the three main networks which want to insure themselves against competition, film production companies, newspaper publishers, the major publishing houses, the main companies which make electronic goods, and even companies which hitherto have been unconnected with the world of the media, such as financial institutions, oil companies and food manufacturers, have all played a part in the expansion of cable and its programmes. While these new entrepreneurs will no doubt be willing to take a certain amount of risks, they will eventually expect to show a profit within a reasonable time, or else they will withdraw their stake and invest elsewhere.

In Europe, political concerns tend to play a part in breaking down the monopolies enjoyed by the public services. But this breakdown is occurring principally against a background in which television is coming to terms with itself as a cultural industry.

Table 1.2 :
Europe's television homes
in millions: 1988

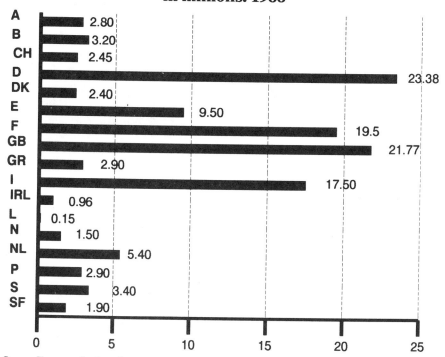

Source: European Institute for the Media, Société européenne des satellites, Cable & Satellite, Kabel & Satellit, Logica.

Until recently Europe has tried to distinguish itself sharply from the United States in its view of television. Over the last two or three generations since the launching of radio services the citizens of most European countries have come to rely on their national governments for the ordering of these services. In return for a monopoly of the medium within the national territory governments exacted requirements regarding the content, quality and character of the services to be provided, and in many countries reserved control of the transmission arrangements to their postal and telegraph administrations. In the 1950's the arrangements governing radio were transferred, with little change, to the emergent television services. It is only since the late 1970's that the relationship between governments and the broadcasting systems has begun to change under the impact of new technologies which have made possible the multiplication of programme services. This evolution is not related directly to the introduction of commercial enterprise into the broadcasting services. A number of national public service systems began to derive revenue from advertising within the framework of their existing statutes. The introduction of the first national television service in Europe financed wholly from advertising revenue, in the United Kingdom in 1954, took place within a framework of statutory accountability similar to the model created for the BBC in 1927. It was conceded that commercial enterprise in the form of advertising revenue might be successfully integrated into the public service model of television in Europe as long as governments retained control of access to broadcast frequencies and were able to contain competition within strict limits.

The developments in broadcasting technology beyond terrestrial transmission to satellite and cable, and the loosening of government control of frequencies have combined with a political climate favourable to deregulation on a broad front to put in question the nature and extent of public accountability in broadcasting. Since the European Television Task Force has concluded that television is a matter for legitimate public concern, it has therefore to spell out the nature of this concern and how it can be met by the exercise of public accountability.

An important new variable in this exercise is the transfrontier character of the emergent television services. In the past governments have been able to order their television systems in their countries in accordance with their sovereign powers, without significant incursions from abroad. In the future this will no longer be possible. As in the case of radio, many television signals will be crossing frontiers. For this reason public accountability, if it is to be effective, must find expression at the European level.

Views differ widely about both the pace of change and the nature of the equilibrium, if any, that will eventually be reached. Existing public service broadcasting organisations tend to minimise the radical nature of the changes that are taking place and emphasise their ability to control the situation. In the United Kingdom for example the BBC and the IBA have claimed that it would be"..well into the 21st century before alternative broadcasting or cable systems posed any threat to the existing duopoly ".[1] These two broadcasting organisations expressed similar views to the Task Force when giving oral evidence, as did the broadcasters and government representatives in Denmark, Norway and Sweden, even though at the time of our visit the

1   Evidence to the Peacock Committee on the future of British broadcasting, 1986

first unauthorised private Swedish television service had begun to transmit programmes to Scandinavia, in the Scandinavian languages, from the United Kingdom. In Belgium, France and the Federal Republic of Germany those giving evidence were already experiencing the early stages of the diversification and deregulation of their television systems, although as yet on a national rather than transnational scale.

Evidence from most other European countries demonstrates the force of the alternative view, that with the proliferation of new commercial broadcasting, cable and satellite channels competing for viewers and viewing time, existing public service channels will find it difficult to retain their present share of television audiences. Their audience figures will tend to fall, both in proportionate and absolute terms. To retain political credibility and to support their case for revenue from public funds, they themselves will be compelled to compete more strongly for mass audiences. Programmes for minority audiences will be either forced off the screen altogether or relegated to off-peak viewing hours. The resulting lack of difference between the programme content of the public service and the private channels will lead to renewed questioning of the need for non-commercial funding of television and perhaps of the very principle of public service television.

A consequence of such a shift towards mass audience programmes will be a predominance of imported programmes, particularly those from the United States, which are generally sold in the European market at lower prices than home-produced material, and could threaten the cultural autonomy of particularly the smaller European countries. For viewers the final paradox would occur if a dramatic increase in channel choice were to result in an effective reduction in the variety of what is on offer at present. There would indeed be more, but more of the same.

At the European political level this development began to be reflected in the work of the Commission of the European Communities which resulted in the publication in 1984 of the Green Paper on Television without Frontiers[1] and the subsequent proposal for a Directive of the Council of Ministers[2]. Although the European Commission denies it, it was an industrial and commercial outlook which led it to declare its intention of establishing a common market in television, as it is doing for goods and other

1   "Television without Frontiers", Commission of the European Communities COM (84) 300 final, 14/6/84
2   Amended Proposal for a Council Directive on the co-ordination of certain provisions laid down by law, regulation or administrative action in Member States concerning the pursuit of broadcasting activities COM (88) 154 final 21/3/88

services. Of course, according to the Green Paper, the circulation of programmes throughout the Community cannot fail to encourage the diversity of European culture and hence to contribute to the process of the unification of Europe. But the principal concerns are undoubtedly economic. It is said, indeed, that the transmission of programmes across frontiers should make a powerful contribution to the development of the Community, in that the advertising which goes with it will make markets larger and more varied. This is discussed more fully in Chapter 4, as is the proposed Convention of the Council of Europe on the same subject.

New Market Structures

In systems of public service television wholly or partly funded by licence fees the sum paid by viewers is related neither to the amount nor to the pattern of their viewing. Where taxation is the source of public funding, the economic relationship between the viewer and the broadcasting organisation or programme maker is even more remote. But perceptions of television as a free (or zero marginal price) service are changing rapidly. As has been pointed out:

" Broadcasting is not, of course, free to the consumer, but it has been, heretofore, free at the point of use. Viewers choosing to watch an individual programme are making choices about the use of their leisure time not about their money. Moves to video, cable, satellite and pay TV, will change the nature of the viewers' decision to ones which include elements of both the use of time and the use of money. These decisions will therefore be more affected by the alternative claims on that time and money both from the individual and their family".[1]

The introduction of a much stronger market element into the relationship between viewers and the supply side of television is likely to have a major impact both on the organisation of the television industry and on programme content. In particular, it will tend to undermine the strong elements of cross-subsidisation — often tacit — that have existed. A pessimistic view is that the decline of cross-subsidisation will mean the end of minority programming in general and especially of cultural programming.

A more optimistic view is that the development of a more direct economic relationship may make the programme makers more responsive to the diverse needs of the viewers. What this will mean in practice will depend very much on the detailed

1   Naomi Sargant, "Learning for TV: the Next Ten Years", a lecture given to the British Royal Society of Arts, 3rd December 1986

8

structure of the market that is created and in particular on the payments systems and technologies that are developed. For example, a pay-per-view system would make it possible to transmit programmes to relatively small audiences composed of consumers willing to pay a relatively large amount to watch a particular programme. Might there not be 500 000 households in Europe willing to pay the equivalent of two ecu each to watch a performance of Siegfried from Bayreuth or a three hour programme on fly-fishing?

From a viewer's perspective, while there are clearly risks in moving towards a market economy in television, there are also potential benefits in developing a system in which consumers can put an economic value on their programme preferences. In the history of television broadcasting organisations, channel providers and programme makers have not shown themselves to be notably sensitive to viewers' preferences and opinions, unless these have supported their struggle for a larger market share. It is conceivable that the discipline of the market, if it can be realised by technologies of payment and the necessary organisational changes, would induce providers to become more responsive to the interests of viewers.

In the view of the European Television Task Force it has to be said that the development of a genuine market in television programming responsive to a wide range of viewers' interests seems less likely than the increasing dominance of restricted markets aimed at limiting viewer choice to a narrow range of programmes calculated to deliver the maximum possible number of home impressions to advertisers.

The restricted markets are of two kinds. First the demand for and supply of television advertising time; and second, the demand for and supply of the goods and services that are advertised on television. It is evident from our meetings with those responsible in the European Commission for the draft Directive on transfrontier broadcasting that it is the needs of these markets which guided the Commission's approach to the creation of the internal market for television within the Community by 1992.

These restricted markets are, of course, legitimate in their own terms. They are restricted in the sense that they tend to distort the real demand for and supply of television programmes. As a recent report by the Consumer and Family Interests in Europe puts it:

" C'est à peine caricaturer que d'affirmer que, dans la plupart des chaînes de type privé, le programme n'existera que comme support d'audience à une autre chose, en l'occurence la publicité".[1]

This incipient distortion of the market is fuelled by the substantial financial prospects that advertising and sponsorship appear to offer not only to commercial channels, but also to governments and some public service broadcasting organisations. In the Task Force's opinion the best means of ensuring that programming in the interests of the people remains dominant in television and that advertising interests play their appropriate, subordinate, role, is to develop direct links between the viewers and the programme providers along the lines suggested. Of course, this will not be the only answer to the problem, but the evidence of consumer expenditure on video recorders and subscriptions to cable channels suggests that viewers are increasingly prepared to pay for their viewing. Increased revenue from viewers is more likely than funding by advertisers to enlarge both the freedom of choice of the consumer and the opportunities available to programme makers to offer a diverse range of programmes to the public.

The outlook for viewer choice on television

During the last few years, both in Europe and in the United States, large holding companies have become interested in communications and within the sector have invested in the audiovisual field and in television, as well as in the press, publishing, records and films, without worrying too much about political frontiers. The profitability of commercial television will henceforth be safeguarded by an expansion of advertising revenue, which in many countries has remained relatively under-exploited, especially on television. To help with the financial stability of the new television stations, governments have generally been more tolerant than they previously were as far as standards of advertising are concerned. In some countries, governments have allowed the proportion of advertising to increase both overall and within each clock-hour of transmission. They are inclined to allow films and other programmes to be interrupted by advertising breaks, whether or not such breaks are "natural". Sponsorship which was previously outlawed, has become standard practice in many instances, bringing with in serious risks of a drift towards the editorial control of advertising.

---

1   BEUC/COFACE "On nous a changé la télé", Brussels 1987. In English this reads: "It is no distortion of the facts to assert that the majority of private television services regard the function of the programmes as being to attract an audience for something else, in effect the advertisements".

In view of the competition which is growing up between many of the parties involved and which, in some countries, has become very keen, it is by no means sure that a concern for quality can always remain uppermost. Except in rare cases, national markets are turning out to be too limited to ensure the profitability of specialised programmes which, in the cultural and linguistic diversity of Europe, have not yet been able to find a wider market. This has meant that so far the main competition has been between programmes with a general appeal of a kind likely to attract the widest public. Rather than make an original programme, producers are tending to use ready-made products of proven effectiveness: films, serials and series, rounded off by variety and chat shows, games and sports spectaculars.

The audiovisual future of Europe is not written in the stars. Whatever a few nostalgic people may want, there is no point in hoping for a return to the reassuring model which held sway for many years when the public services predominated on the national scene. Even so, systematic deregulation placing its faith in the free play of economic forces is not desirable; it could not in any way guarantee that the competitive struggle for advertising markets would produce real diversification or that more interesting programmes would follow. Nor is it certain that the extension of a system by which all programmes would be paid for by subscription or on a "pay-per-view" basis could in every case be sufficient to make them profitable.

The European Television Task Force takes the view that, between a return to the authoritarianism of the public service monopolies and the anarchy which would result from unbridled competition, there is a third way. This option would enable organisations with a different legal status and financed in different ways to co-exist, bringing real diversity into the content and spirit of programmes, accepting responsibilities over and above the search for immediate profit, and accepting certain minimum operating standards within a European framework. It is within such a framework that the relationship of the European citizens to their television services should evolve.

Chapter 2
The new European audiovisual landscape

Television and technical change

Since its inception, television has been the mass-communications medium most closely linked to technology. Many scientific disciplines have contributed to its development: mechanics, electronics, optics, acoustics and many others. But, during the last ten years, its rapid evolution has been determined by the technology of semiconductors, lasers, fibre optics and space.

Semiconductors, in particular, have given rise to integrated circuits ("chips") and to micro-processors. With striking rapidity, these devices have achieved higher and higher levels of performance, in their capacity to store data, their computation speed and their complexity. At the same time their dimensions, their energy consumption and their relative cost have constantly fallen. Hence it has proved possible to use digital data processing for television, and this is the basis of the explosive development of the electronic computer industry. All that was required was the conversion into digital data sequences of the series of images and sounds captured analogically by the television camera and the microphone. The combination of digital methods, integrated circuits and micro-processors has revolutionised every aspect of television technology, whether it be the production, processing, storage, transmission, broadcasting or receiving of audiovisual information. Its most spectacular effect has been to multiply considerably the number of television programmes which can be distributed in Europe, as a result, particularly, of developments in cable and satellite.

From now on, the networks of land-based transmitters and cabling systems can be developed more economically than in the past. Within the foreseeable future laser and fibre optic technology will make it possible to increase the capacity of cable systems to such an extent that the number of television programmes being distributed − at the same time as other telecommunications services − will probably be limited by economic rather than technical considerations. The development of wide-band integrated service digital networks (ISDN) and the *RACE* programme of the European

Commission to establish such a network on a European scale will be important milestones on this road.

Finally, geostationary satellites make it possible to gather and transmit audiovisual events as they happen and from any part of the world. These so-called "fixed service satellites" also carry programmes intended for eventual delivery by cable. Despite the stipulations of the Radio Regulations issued by the International Telecommunication Union (ITU), which place this service in the "confidential" category and do not regard it as broadcasting, several governments have authorised the reception by the general public, and without encrypting, of programmes emanating from these satellites. Hence the opportunities for receiving them are greatly increased. Higher-powered satellites of this kind have already been announced: today the best known of them is the ASTRA satellite belonging to the Luxemburg company Société européenne des satellites (SES), and scheduled for launching in 1989.

The "direct broadcast" satellites whose transmitters operate in the 12GHz band are even more powerful, and this makes it possible for individuals to receive them using small-size inexpensive dish antennae From 1989 onwards, satellites of this kind will be making their appearance: TDF1 (France), TV-SAT (Federal Republic of Germany), OLYMPUS (European Space Agency, Italy, EBU), TELE-X (Scandinavian countries) and BSB (United Kingdom). Since their transmitters are located at a very high altitude (some 36 km above the Equator), the satellites cover most of the European countries, without being in the least hampered by political frontiers.

For this reason, they cannot be subject to purely national regulations, as traditional terrestrial broadcasting transmitters were for many years. The development of technology is also producing a plethora of new kinds of equipment, methods and systems which affect the audiovisual material from the point of its origination to the moment it is finally seen by the viewer in the home.

A few examples may be useful:

● Television cameras are no longer heavy and cumbersome; portable versions are regularly used for news reports (ENG = Electronic News Gathering) and even for the production of drama (EFR = Electronic Field Production).

● Professional-quality recording equipment is developing along the same lines.

- Digital image processing allows virtually limitless possibilities for manipulating and altering pictures, as well as for creating entirely artificial images.

- The digital television studio will exist before long, and the first digital video and audio recorders, which are regarded as the major feature of such studios, are now on the market.

- Electronic production of a quality equivalent to that of 35mm cinema films, is becoming possible thanks to high-definition television techniques.

- The new transmission systems which conform to the MAC-Packet range of standards offer better-quality images and sound, as well as additional services such as multiple sound-tracks.

- These systems are likely to develop into a high-definition television broadcasting system, which should provide images and communication of exceptionally high quality.

- Teletext services are being perfected; they are gradually being introduced in every country in Europe.

- The transmission of stereophonic sound or of two sound tracks transmitted in parallel will become usual; this procedure, like teletext, may make it easier to cross linguistic barriers.

- The encrypting of images and sound will make it possible to introduce pay-television.

- The broadcasting of auxiliary signals, which are invisible on the viewer's screen, will make it possible, among other things, to automate the recording of programmes at home.

- Recording equipment designed for the mass market allows viewers to decide what to watch, either by hiring or buying videograms on cassette or on video-disc, or by recording the programmes transmitted by cable or over the air.

All the equipment and systems listed above require common technical standards to be established if the common market for television is to become a reality. In some cases, this standardisation is already happening at the European level, and even world-wide. But, in others, some organisations and some national industries are not waiting for European standards to be established before they exploit the new technologies. The European Television Task Force takes the view that this trend is dangerous. It recommends that every effort should be made to bring about the standardisation and harmonisation of technical systems. In particular, it recommends the adoption, for television satellite broadcasting, of a single technical standard, of a kind which would be likely to bring about high-definition television. The Task Force considers that it is desirable, in addition, that European manufacturers should try to market television receivers capable of receiving signals emanating from land-based transmitters as well as cable and satellite signals. As far as encryption is concerned, we believe that a common system, or at the very least a group of compatible systems, should be developed. Restricted-access television systems should be legally protected against illicit reception, and this protection should be harmonised at the European level. The opportunities offered by technology should be exploited to enable the European public to receive a wide variety of services and programmes in the language of its choice.

In conclusion, it may be noted that the major consequences of the development of technology, especially in the last ten years, have been as follows:

- a broadening and an expansion of production methods which are likely to reduce production costs and to lead to the appearance on the market of new companies and producers;

- a broadening of content within television transmission channels and especially a very large increase in the number of television channels as a result of the development of cable systems, satellites and videograms.

Changes in the structures of television.

The trend towards deregulation.

The development of the European audiovisual scene is characterised not only by technological advances which have made possible a great increase in the number of transmission sources. In response to the wishes of private groups and of some sectors of public opinion, many states have abolished the public service monopoly which had previously been the organisational framework for broadcasting in most countries from the inception of television. This monopoly was based on the bringing together, to a greater or lesser degree depending on the country concerned, of three ideas:

- **a transmission monopoly:** the national post and telecommunications services, specialised organisations (such as TDF in France) or the public broadcasting services themselves had a technical monopoly of broadcasting;

- **a programming monopoly:** in most States, only the public service broadcasting organisations were authorised to offer programme services to the public, and these services were financed to varying degrees by the licence-fee or by advertising;

- **a production monopoly:** in some countries, the public service broadcasters, either by law or in fact, themselves produced the majority of their programmes, especially drama, or else were obliged to have them made by public service organisations which worked specially for them (for example, the SFP in France, and the NOS facilities in the Netherlands).

These three forms of monopoly have now ceased to exist in most European countries.

The monopoly of **transmission** is certainly the one which remains the most firmly established. However, in many countries, private companies have been given permission to use the cable networks (Belgium, the Netherlands, Switzerland and, more recently, the United Kingdom, France, Spain and Ireland), or local terrestrial broadcasting stations (Italy, France), and even to set up terrestrial broadcasting stations for transmitting national channels (France). What is more, the agreement signed in September 1987 between EUTELSAT and the Société européenne des satellites, which will launch the ASTRA satellite in 1988, ends the European PTT monopoly of the application of space telecommunications to television.

If one accepts the most widely-favoured interpretation of Article 10 of the European Convention on Human Rights, the **programming** monopoly no longer exists, legally speaking, in the states which are party to the Convention. Of course, in some countries, the state still, in fact, reserves the public service concession for public corporations alone (some of the Länder in the German Federal Republic, Austria, Greece, Ireland, Norway, Portugal, Sweden, Turkey). But the lifting of the programming monopoly in many states (most of the German Länder, Belgium, France, Italy, Denmark, Switzerland, Iceland) is the most important feature of the last few years. The lifting of the programming monopoly is also on the agenda in Spain, Greece, the Netherlands, Norway and Portugal). While the particular situation varies greatly from one country to another, it is however possible to list briefly the various types to be found:

Countries with long-established dual systems

Since 1953 and 1954 respectively, Finland and Great Britain have had a dual system, based on competition conducted within a framework of public control between the public service organisations and the commercial broadcasters. The British model has often been cited elsewhere to justify the view that the time has come to abolish regulation. But the commercial broadcasters in the United Kingdom have had public service obligations placed upon them by the legislature. Their selection and their observance of the contracts awarded to them has been the duty of a public Authority. But, with the setting up of Channel 4 in 1981, the authorisation given in 1984 for specific services to be supplied by cable, the suggestion that the BBC should be financed on a "pay as you view" basis, the suggestion that a fifth terrestrial channel should be launched and the authorisation of additional channels to be transmitted by direct broadcast satellite, the traditional model is undergoing considerable change.

Smaller countries with a private sector monopoly

Two states (the Grand-Duchy of Luxemburg and the Principality of Monaco) grasped at an early stage that the time was ripe to offer a haven for the pioneers of commercial transfrontier television financed by advertising: the CLT and Tele Monte Carlo. This policy of making them welcome has enabled these companies to offer programmes (and advertising) to neighbouring countries (Belgium, Eastern France, and the Federal Republic of Germany in the case of the CLT, the South of France and Italy in the case of Tele Monte Carlo). The European ambitions demonstrated by the CLT at the end of the 1970's put Luxemburg in particular at the centre of the questions posed by transfrontier television.

Smaller densely-cabled countries with heavy penetration by foreign services

In Belgium, the Netherlands, Switzerland, and to a lesser extent in Denmark and in Ireland, interest in the services emanating from larger neighbouring countries was the initial cause of the development of the cable networks which put an end to the monopoly enjoyed by the national public service organisations. It is a paradox, though an understandable one, that the governments of these smaller states were for many years disinclined to authorise powerful national commercial channels. The legal breaking of the monopoly was initially effected on a small scale, through the authorising of local stations with a socio-cultural purpose (the French community in Belgium, and in Switzerland and Denmark) and of pay-television (Switzerland, Denmark, and the Flemish community in Belgium). The setting up of national commercial channels, financed by advertising and with restrictive charters, has been authorised in Belgium and Denmark only since 1987. In the Netherlands and in Switzerland, the setting up of such channels has been considered, but it is unlikely to come about in the short term.

The challenge of deregulatory processes

The three countries concerned are Italy, France and the Federal Republic of Germany. Although these processes differ widely from one country to another, important similarities can be discerned:

- competition was initiated by making the public service compete within itself (three public service channels, the third of which was mainly regionally oriented);

- during the 1970's, the forces of political opposition (the Socialist and Communist parties in France and Italy, and the Christian-Democrats in the Federal Republic of Germany) challenged the political hegemony over the public service broadcasters enjoyed by the parties in power;

- the absence of a minimal degree of consensus between the political parties about the way in which the systems should be managed was complicated by the constitutional structures of the countries: the absence of, or disagreement about, the broadcasting law in Italy, the upheavals caused by changes in the political majority in France, and the devolution of responsibilty for the media to eleven regional governments in the Federal Republic of Germany. These factors brought about rapid change which had not been adequately prepared;

- the difficulty of formulating a political consensus led the highest legal bodies (the Council of State, and the Constitutional Courts) to play an important part in defining a legal framework for broadcasting based on the factual realities of the situation;

- the difficulty experienced by the public service organisations and the private sector in arriving at a *modus vivendi* for harmonious competition is centred on a few key facts and ideas, the most important of which are: the sharing of advertising resources; the creation of national terrestrial broadcasting networks for the new services; the inflation of programme costs; a policy for access to satellites; freedom from government control, particularly in the area of news; and the formulation of new rules for audience measurement;

- deregulation makes possible the formation of powerful multimedia groups, whose ambitions transcend national frontiers: Silvio Berlusconi's FININVEST group (3 channels in Italy and a shareholding in La Cinq in France), the newspaper groups such as Axel Springer, Bertelsmann and others, together with the Leo Kirch group in the Federal Republic of Germany, the Bouygues and Hersant groups in France, and the CLT in France, in Belgium and the Federal Republic of Germany.

Countries in which the public service monopoly remains intact

In a few European countries the public service monopoly is still in operation in practice, even if it is being challenged on legal or doctrinal grounds. In the medium term, it is likely that in these countries the television system will, under pressure from international trends, also move in the direction of deregulation. In Spain and Portugal the setting up of commercial channels is now officially on the agenda, and is forecast for 1990. In Norway and Sweden, it is intended that competition should be provided through the setting up of new public service channels, financed if need be through advertising. Countries in which it does not appear that new channels will be set up in the immediate future are Austria, Greece and Turkey.

Finally, the **production monopoly** itself is disappearing. In France and in the Netherlands, the regulations which required broadcasters to use the public service infrastructures (SFP, NOS) to make their programmes have been abolished. In Great Britain, Channel 4 was designed to be an organisation using outside producers. It makes only 1% of its own programmes and places orders with independent producers for much of its output. The promotion of independent production has become one of the features common to the audiovisual policies pursued by a number of organisations including the BBC, which has been known for its rigorous policy of producing its own programmes internally. By making it obligatory for broadcasters to devote 5% (rising to 10%) of their programme budget to independent productions, the European Commission's proposed Directive confirms this trend.

The internationalisation of European television transmissions

Alongside the process of deregulation which is taking place at the national level, television is now faced with a process of internationalisation which takes many forms: deliberate overspill across frontiers, international collaboration in the setting up of transfrontier services, foreign groups having a stake in the capital of national services, the search for an international advertising market, and the development of co-production or co-financing in the production of programmes.Transfrontier broadcasting is the most remarkable, and the most problematic, form taken by this process of internationalisation. It has several features which deserve comment.

Natural overspill

For obvious physical reasons, ground-based over-the-air broadcasting cannot be limited by frontiers. There have always been natural overspills; these were inevitable and were of little concern to the national stations operating in the countries affected.

Land-based television stations transmitting to neighbouring countries

The deliberate transmission of terrestrial broadcasts to neighbouring countries poses rather more problems, as is demonstrated particularly by the case of RTL which, thanks to cable, was widely received in Belgium. This diverted to the Grand-Duchy of Luxemburg the money which Belgian firms invested in advertising, thereby making the public service channel of the French-speaking community in Belgium its competitor and creating conflict between them. This text-book example, since resolved by the establishment of a Belgian company, TVi, with substantial participation from RTL's parent company CLT, explains why a number of states have adopted protectionist attitudes in seeking a legal framework for broadcasting in Europe.

Relays of foreign domestic services

The relaying of foreign channels within a given country is nowadays the most frequent form of transfrontier broadcasting. The relay is usually by means of cable and, less frequently, via terrestrial relay networks (for example Antenne 2 and Tele Monte Carlo in Italy, the Finnish channel YLE in Sweden). Satellites can also be used for such transmissions (as is the case with the RAI, SVT, BBC and others).

Table 2.1:
TV services in Europe broadcast by low power satellite

Service	Hours per day	Language	House holds	Source of Finance	Ownership
3-SAT	8	German	3 432 280	Advertising	ZDF/ORF/SRG
AFRTS	24	English	See note[1]	US Govt	US Government
Arts Channel	3	English	3 000[2]	Advertising	WH Smith, TVS, Commercial Union, Equity & Law
BBC1/2 mix	8	English	na	Fees from cable	BBC
BR3	10	German	1 900 000[3]	Licence fee	Bayerischer Runfunk
Canal 10	24	Spanish	na	Advertising	FININVEST, Thorn EMI
Childrens Channel	10	English	887 000	Advertising	British Telecom, DC Thomson, Thames, Central TV, Thorn EMI
CNN	24	English	233 209	Advertising	Turner B'casting
Eins Plus	4-5	German	2 860 000[3]	Licence fee	ARD
Eureka	12-18	German	2 520 000[3]	Advertising	Medi-Media GmbH
FilmNet	24	Dutch[4]	65 000	Subscription	Esselte, UIP, VNU
Info Film	various	Norwegian	na	download fees[5]	na
Kindernet	3	Dutch	60 000	Fee from Cable Operators	Telecable Benelux, WH Smith, Fuji 8
La Cinq	17	French	92 150[6]	Advertising	Fininvest, Hersant
Lifestyle	6	English	203 300	Advertising	WH Smith, TVS, Yorkshire TV, DC Thomson

1   Service restricted to American Forces in Germany
2   Source Cable & Satellite Europe February 1988. The Arts Channel programme is transmitted on the same channel as, and immediately following closedown of, Sky Channel.
3   Households in the FRG only.
4   FilmNet also carries programming in Scandinavian languages, principally Swedish.
5   Info Film offers privately produced programmes for download to Norwegian local tv stations.
6   60% of France can receive La Cinq either by satellite or terrestrial transmission

M6	16	French	20 780	Advertising	CLT, Compagnie Lyonnaise des Eaux
MTV	24	English	2 212 425	Advertising.	Maxwell Comms
NRK	9	Norwegian	10 000	NRK	NRK
Premiere	12	English	40 000[1]	Subscription	Maxwell, Columbia 20th Fox, HBO, Showtime/The Movie Channel
RAI Uno	18	Italian	1 500 000[2]	RAI	RAI
RTL Plus	7	German	2 868 280	Advertising	CLT, Bertelsmann
SAT I	12	German	2 873 280	Advertising	PKS (Kirch 51%, DG Bank 49%) APF, Springer, Von Holtzbrink
Screensport	9	English	241 110	Advertising & Subscription	WH Smith, ESPN, ABC, RCA 3i's
SKY Channel	19	English	10 869 773	Advertising	News International, Ferranti, Ladbroke, DC Thomson, Equity & Law
Super Channel	20	English	9 660 000	Advertising	UK ITV exc. Thames & TVam, Virgin
SVT1 & 2	14	Swedish	na	na	SVT
Teleclub[3]	6	German	30 000	Subscription	Beta Taurus
Tele-Fünf	24	German	2 860 000[4]	Advertising	KMP/ FININVEST
TV3 (Scansat)	6	Swedish/ Danish/ Norwegian	850 (1987)	Advertising	Kinnevik (96%) & Nora (4%)
TV5	7	French	7 029 685	na	TF1,A2,FR3,SSR, RTBF, CTQC
TVE1 (Spain)	18	Spanish	na	TVE	RTVE
WEST 3	10	German	1 900 000[4]	WDR	Westdeustcher Rundfunk
Worldnet	5	English	3 452 212	US Government	USIA.

Source: European Institute for the Media/ Prestel Satellite Informer

1   Source "Cable & Satellite Europe" February 1988
2   In 1987
3   The Teleclub service ceased operations early in 1988
4   Households in FRG only

Transfrontier services transmitted by satellite

Communications satellites have made it possible to set up services aimed entirely or in part at the European market. In 1987, some 27 transfrontier services were already transmitting to Europe; another ten or so are already being planned. When direct broadcast satellites are launched there will be even more services in Europe.

The internationalisation of investment

The phenomenon of foreign investment in the capital of broadcasting companies is not new, but is tending to become widespread. The CLT (Compagnie luxembourgeoise de télédiffusion) has been a pioneer in the European audiovisual industry. After broadcasting for many years to neighbouring countries from transmitters within the Grand-Duchy of Luxemburg, CLT has now become involved directly in the ownership and management of national companies based in, and broadcasting within, the countries concerned: France, the Federal Republic of Germany and Belgium. With close links to the Compagnie Bruxelles-Lambert, itself part of the Swiss-based Pargesa Holding conglomerate with interestes throughout the world, CLT is diversifying into production and distribution in the cinema and record industries.

CLT now has many competitors, including Silvio Berlusconi's FININVEST Group, with interests in publishing and the cinema, and which owns three television channels in Italy as well as having interests in television in France, the Federal Republic of Germany and in Canada; the Maxwell Communications Corporation of the United Kingdom, a subsidiary of the Pergamon Foundation, which has interests especially in newspapers and in publishing, but also owns a number of cable and satellite television companies in Great Britain, as well as a stake in French television, and wishes to gain a foothold elsewhere; News International, owned by Rupert Murdoch, which is active in cable television and in satellite broadcasting in Europe (Sky Channel and the new EBU sports service), as well as in Australia and in the United States. Other powerful groups, which in some of their communications activities (such as the press, publishing and the cinema) already have interests in Europe, are for the moment basing themselves on television in their own countries, but are preparing to expand elsewhere when the opportunity presents itself include: Bertelsmann, Hachette, Agence Havas, Hersant, Axel Springer and the Virgin group.

The national laws dealing with private television stations in the member States of the European Community generally permit investments originating from other member States, provided reciprocal arrangements exist. The draconian limitations which are enshrined in certain laws opposed to these provisions (the decree issued by the Flemish community in Belgium on 28 January 1987, the bill published in Spain in April 1987 dealing with commercial television, the Portuguese law dealing with the press) appear to have no validity, and it is doubtful whether they conform to the Treaty of Rome. However, some precautions should be taken. Indeed, through their large shareholdings in television management companies in a number of countries, industrial and financial groups constitute true multimedia multinational companies, in which the powers which they exercise over television and its programmes are combined with their influence over radio, the press, book and record publishing and the cinema. Of course, if audiovisual communication is to make itself felt as a major sector of the economy, it needs powerful groups in Europe to represent it. The Task Force takes the view that limitations should be placed on economic concentration, to prevent groups achieving positions of dominance which might lead to the misuse of their power and endanger pluralism and the freedom of information.

Such limitations already exist in some countries. At the European level, specific legal provisions will be required in addition to the guarantees offered in this area by articles 85 and 86 of the Treaty of Rome, as well as by the guarantees provided by article 10 of the European Convention on Human Rights. This topic is explored in greater detail in Chapter 4.

Finally, the acquisition of a majority shareholding in broadcasting companies by non-European shareholders will need to be considered carefully. In this connection, it will be noted that national laws (and especially the Cable and Broadcasting Act passed in 1984 in the United Kingdom) are more liberal than American legislation, which restricts the possibility of foreign shareholding in a communications company to 25% of its capital. This is a point on which the European authorities will need to move carefully, especially in anticipation of the negotiations which will be taking place on these matters under the auspices of GATT and the OECD.

Although the general trends are common to all countries considerable variations exist from one country to another so far as the application of broadcasting technologies and the institutional arrangements for ending the public service monopolies are concerned; hence, there are also considerable variations in the programmes available.Before gauging the effects of, and the prospects for, transfrontier broadcasting (and so far this has had a marked effect on only a small number of countries), it is appropriate to use a few examples to illustrate the changes which are taking place even within national contexts.

Competition in a national context

The United Kingdom

Since 1954 the United Kingdom has experienced competition between a public service (the **BBC**) funded mainly from the licence fee, and the commercial television stations, which are financed through advertising. The struggle between the two sides may indeed have led to keen competition for audiences; but they have usually respected the proprieties and adhered to common rules. This was made all the easier by the fact that commercial television has always been subject to, and monitored by, a public authority, the **Independent Broadcasting Authority**. This body allocates to commercial companies, for a specified period, the right to transmit, in a given region, on certain days and at certain times, programmes which are financed from the sale of advertising. The IBA, though producing no programmes itself, has wide powers over the programme schedules as a whole and for seeing that individual programmes do not contravene the governing statute. Because the legal, regulatory or customary provisions are quite strict, the various broadcasting companies, for their part, are obliged to adhere to precise criteria in such matters as advertising, programme quality, the country of origin of programmes (subject to certain exceptions not more than 14% should originate outside the European Community) and the impartiality of news programmes.

The fourth channel (**Channel 4**) is a subsidiary of the IBA; it secures its programmes from outside producers and mainly caters for minority audiences. Channel 4 does not sell its own advertising but receives a proportion, determined by the IBA, of the revenues of the various commercial members of the ITV system. In 1988 this proportion is 17% which covers the Welsh 4th channel also.

From the outset, the United Kingdom system has been tempered by a number of regulations which have been applied in a public service spirit, both by the commercial companies monitored by the IBA and by the BBC. The beginnings of a change became discernible in 1983 with the passing of a law permitting the establishment of local cable systems with the aim of establishing on a more diversified basis a form of competition which would not, however, develop in an anarchic way. Cable franchises are awarded to operators on the basis of their development plans, by a Cable Authority which sets standards and monitors their application. The cable systems are financed by subscription or by advertising. The franchises relate to local audiences but may use signals transmitted by satellite to the whole country. Cable programmes have a mainly thematic character based on films, music or sport. For the time being, they are not a threat to the general-interest channels of the BBC and the IBA, since cable is still very underdeveloped in Great Britain.

The Federal Republic of Germany

In the Federal Republic of Germany the long-standing opposition shown by those Länder controlled by Social Democrat Governments towards commercial television (the constitution of the Federal Republic gives the Länder responsibility for broadcasting) means that competition between the public and the private sectors has not yet reached its full potential. The television system is still based mainly on regional public service broadcasting organisations which are responsible to the Länder and which co-operate within the **ARD**, and on a public broadcasting organisation which is common to all the Länder and which provides the second television channel (**ZDF**). But the system has been called in question ever since the Constitutional Court allowed the duality of the public-private system to be recognised in the audiovisual sphere, and since a Federal treaty guaranteed the development of commercial stations over the whole country as well as the maintenance of the funds allocated to the public service broadcasters.

Among the services transmitted by cable can be found local programmes, thematic programmes based especially on music, two satellite channels financed from public funds, **3-SAT** (produced by the ZDF, Austrian television (ORF) and the Swiss television service (SRG); and **Eins Plus,** launched by the ARD in preparation for the launching of direct broadcast satellite. But the keenest competition which the ARD and the ZDF have to face comes from two general-interest commercial stations which also transmit by terrestrial broadcasting: **SAT 1** and **RTL Plus** which are backed by powerful industrial and commercial interests. These two channels are indeed bringing a new spirit and new methods to the German television scene. As they rely entirely on advertising, they are constantly trying to attract the largest possible audience and their programmes are designed to achieve this aim. The area they cover is still limited — as yet they reach only about 3 million homes — but their presence is already making it necessary for the Federal Republic of Germany to seek a new balance, which will probably be more difficult to achieve and less harmonious than that which has hitherto held sway.

The Italian experience

Italy is the country which has probably undergone the most dramatic upheavals in the audiovisual sphere in the last few years. Commercial television there originates from a judgement which ruled that the monopoly enjoyed by the public broadcasting organisation, the **RAI**, was unconstitutional at the local level. Local television stations, transmitting first by cable then by terrestrial means used the available frequencies to cover limited geographical areas: these numbered more than 1 200 in 1982. Since that time, the number has fallen, most of the commercial stations now being incorporated into major networks covering the whole country. The three main ones (**Canale 5, Italia 1** and **Rete 4**) are controlled by Silvio Berlusconi's FININVEST group. Until new legislation (which is taking a long time to materialise) comes into force, commercial television stations are legally allowed to operate only at local level; consequently, their output can be linked up only by means of the simultaneous transmission of pre-recorded tapes, although this has not impeded their success.

As a result, television advertising in Italy has really taken off. Whereas the RAI was subject to laws which restricted the opportunities it could offer, the private sector recognises no regulations. It has relentlessly increased the duration of advertising time, especially at peak viewing periods, and has not hesitated to interrupt its programmes on a massive scale with numerous advertisements. The three main Berlusconi channels have captured some 60% of the money invested in an expanding advertising market; the RAI has about 30% and the other stations have the rest. The commercial success of the private sector is due to a programme policy which aims systematically to maximise the viewing figures.

On the commercial networks 70 to 75% of the schedules are made up of cinema films, series, TV films and cartoons. To obtain material the private sector soon turned to programmes produced in foreign countries, and especially the United States where there is an abundance of programmes which have already recouped their cost on the home market. As far as existing stocks were concerned, this material could initially be acquired cheaply; competition between buyers has resulted in the price of the most popular productions rising considerably. Even so, the purchase of ready-made products remains much less expensive than the production of original dramatic works. However FININVEST has started to produce a number of these in the last few years. The private television channels fill their schedules with game shows (in which the public can win large sums of money), variety shows with famous stars, and sporting coverage.

In order to maintain its popularity with viewers, the RAI has had to outbid other channels to acquire film series, cinema films, and the rights to sporting events, and to retain popular personalities who can attract the largest audience. It has been led to change its schedules completely, modifying the time allocated to the various types of programmes which it transmits, giving a larger share to spectaculars, variety shows, games, films and series. It has reduced the allocation given to educational and strictly cultural programmes. This does not mean that the RAI has abandoned its public service obligations. It is active on the news front, where it maintains[3]has given rise to much controversy. Although it has greatly increased the number of programmes with low production costs such as talk shows, it has managed to invest in the production of original drama, either in co-production with the film industry or with a number of American network producers.

After a period of instability, the Italian television scene should become somewhat less hectic. The excesses of advertising have become such that the public is growing tired of them. There is now talk of a "mixed system" in which a balance would be struck between the public service and the commercial organisations. After an utterly anarchic process of deregulation, a need is being felt for a structure which will guarantee the legal existence of commercial television not only at the local, but at the national level; and which will, in return, impose a number of qualitative obligations on it. The Government will have to decide whether to intervene in the matter.

The new audiovisual scene in France

In France a different kind of competition has emerged in the last few years. The change began in 1974 with the separation of the ORTF into three distinct channels, but these — which were financed both by licence-fees and by advertising revenue — were still public institutions with well defined aims and detailed charters. Since that time, TF1 has been privatised, two commercial services — **La Cinq** and **M6** — have come into being and the **Canal Plus** pay-channel, which relies mainly on films is enjoying substantial success.

Cable remains at the embryo stage; the new television services are using networks of terrestrial broadcasting transmitters which are gradually being extended to cover the whole country. The increased number of channels is therefore the result, essentially, of a political decision which took account both of the public desire for a wider choice of programmes, and of economic pressure from those who wished to take advantage of advertising resources in a sector which was still underdeveloped in France.

The competition which is growing up among the services has features in common with those which have been noted in Italy. It affects first and foremost programmes which have a guaranteed audience: variety and game shows, repeats of sports programmes, films, drama series and imported TV films. In a short time costs have increased in all these categories. The desire to outbid rivals has become apparent also in the hunt for stars, not only to compere variety and game shows, but also to present television news programmes. Even though the receipts from advertising are expanding greatly, the increase in costs of the kinds of programmes which attract large audiences reduces the resources available for minority programmes, especially those of a cultural kind.

In many respects, however, the situation in France is different from that in Italy. The commercial organisations are obliged to accept a number of obligations laid down by the authorities. In order to secure the right to transmit programmes, they have had to assume additional responsibilities Of course, these conditions are less onerous than those required of the publicly-funded channels (**A2** and **FR3**), but they are not negligible. They relate to advertising standards, to the way in which films are transmitted, the obligation to use independent producers, and quotas for the production of original programmes. After the short period during which the system has been operating, it is still uncertain whether the statutory monitoring body, the *Commission nationale de la Communication et des Libertés* (CNCL) will have the resources to ensure that commitments are respected and to exact sanction for any failure to do so.

Changes in Viewer behaviour

In Chapter 1 we have discussed the role of television in the lives of the people in general. Here the Task Force deals with one particular aspect of viewer behaviour arising from the changes in the European audiovisual landscape. This is access to television programmes originating outside the viewer's country.

Until now the increase in the number of services and the development of competition among the services has occurred mainly at the national level. Changes in the behaviour of viewers have been linked to the commercial nature of the new television stations and to the dominant role which they have given to entertainment in their programmes. Only the most densely-cabled countries have any continuous experience, on a reasonably wide scale, of the reception of foreign services.

Table 2.2:Cable penetration in Europe in 1987

(as a percentage of television households)

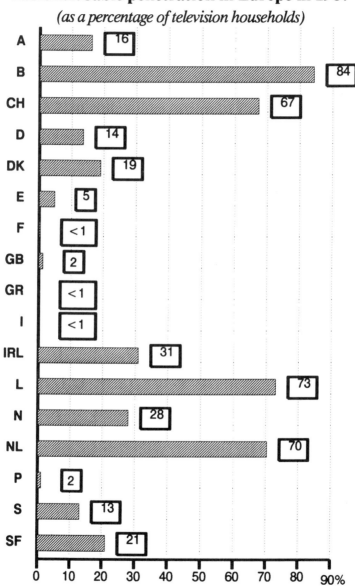

Source: National sources, compiled by European Institute for the Media

Viewers and foreign services

Depending on the level of cabling, it is possible to distinguish three categories of countries in Europe (see Table 2.2):

- densely-cabled countries: Belgium (over 84%), the Netherlands (70%), and Switzerland (nearly 70%); between the three of them, these countries account for 60% of the European homes connected to the cable networks;

- countries with an average amount of cabling (between 14% and 50%): Denmark, Finland, the Federal Republic of Germany, Ireland and Norway;

- countries with little or no cabling (less than 13%): France, Greece, Italy, Portugal, Spain, Sweden and the United Kingdom.

These percentages must be modified to the extent that in some countries – especially the United Kingdom and Ireland – the number of cable subscribers is as yet far below the number of installations which can be connected to cable, either because the cost of the subscription is discouraging, or because the programmes offered are not thought to be sufficiently attractive.

The experience of Belgium and the Netherlands

In Belgium and the Netherlands, the cable networks already distribute some twenty programmes emanating from the national transmitters of foreign countries, as well as a few programmes transmitted by satellite. The capacity of the networks may be increased still further.

In the Netherlands, in 1980, 89% of the time devoted to television involved watching the Dutch national services. In 1986, despite the great increase in the number of foreign services available on cable, the national services still made a better showing, with 84% of the audience time. The most noteworthy change is connected with the coming of **Sky Channel**, an English language satellite service which offers non-stop light entertainment. This channel accounts only for 5% of the overall viewing time; the German-language programmes transmitted by the **ARD** and the **ZDF** account for another 5%, and the programmes in Dutch by the neighbouring **BRT** channel also account for 5%; the rest (including French-language programmes) account for 1%.

Table 2.3 : Audience fragmentation by language preference in densely cabled European countries

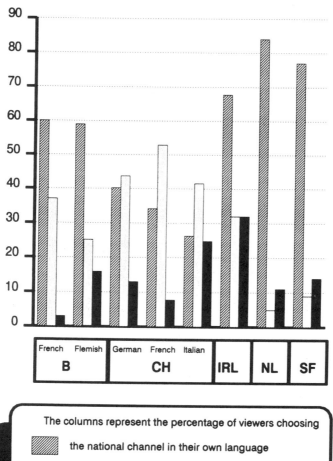

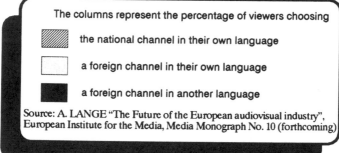

The columns represent the percentage of viewers choosing

▨ the national channel in their own language

☐ a foreign channel in their own language

■ a foreign channel in another language

Source: A. LANGE "The Future of the European audiovisual industry",
European Institute for the Media, Media Monograph No. 10 (forthcoming)

All the foreign-language programmes together account, therefore, for only 11% of viewing time.

In Flemish-speaking Belgium the BRT channels attract 59% of the audience, and the Dutch-language channels emanating from the Netherlands take 25%. The French-language channels (three French, two Belgian, and one Luxemburgish) take 11% in all, while the German-language channels take 3%. All the non-Dutch channels together therefore attract viewers for only 16% of the time.

In the French Community of Belgium, the French-language television channel transmitting from Luxemburg, RTL, was for many years the most formidable competitor to the RTBF; but since 1987, RTL has become a participant in the Belgian commercial channel, TVi. The competition which it has always offered must therefore now be considered at the level of the internal rivalry between public and commercial organisations. The French-language Belgian channels together account today for 60% of viewing time; the foreign French-language channels (three French channels and, playing a minor role, the French-language channel transmitted by the TV5 satellite) have 37%, and channels using other languages (including the Flemish-language Belgian channels) a mere 3%. In other countries too — especially in Finland, Germany, Ireland, and Switzerland— studies based on more limited experiments have been undertaken into how viewers react to the increase in the number of programmes available. Table 2.3 sets out the viewer preferences in five countries.

It is noticeable, (and see Table 1.1), that an increase in the range of programmes does not fundamentally alter the habits of viewers: the average time devoted to television does not increase in accordance with the number of channels, but only insofar as the additional programmes are sufficiently new and attractive and also, particularly, if they are transmitted at times which are not already accounted for.

Reactions to foreign languages

It is undeniable that, as a general rule, foreign languages act as a disincentive, but it is not equally marked in every area and in every country. The reaction of the cinema-going public to the dubbing and sub-titling of films is well known: in France, Germany, Italy, the United Kingdom,and the United States the public, except for a small minority, prefers to see films dubbed. This is the case in every country which uses a widely-spoken language, and which has a wide range of films in its own language at its disposal. French-speaking Belgium conforms to this model. Elsewhere, sub-titling is more readily accepted: in Flanders, the Netherlands, and in the Scandinavian countries the fact that there is not a sufficiently large range of films in the national language and that the cost of dubbing for a restricted market is too high, has conditioned the public to accept sub-titling. It is accepted on television as in the cinema, even if it is harder to read.

But many foreign-language programmes on television are not translated at all. From surveys carried out the knowledge of foreign languages claimed by the citizens of the various countries of Europe it appears that the actual viewing figures for programmes in these languages are far smaller than the numbers who claim to understand them.Some programmes seem able to dispense easily with verbal explanation. Sport is one example: sports enthusiasts find to their delight that foreign services are showing competitions in sports with which they are unfamiliar, such as snooker, darts, rugby and American football. But in the case of sports which concern them more directly, they want the pictures to be accompanied by a commentary which links them with what they see, and a commentator to intervene to draw attention to the achievements of those taking part.

The language of the music used on variety shows aimed at young people is mainly Anglo-American in origin, and appears to be generally understood. But it appeals only to a certain age-group. Other variety shows, even when they feature famous stars, usually need comperes who achieve popularity only within a homogeneous linguistic area. Opera, symphonic music, and the major soloists may also find an audience which transcends frontiers, but the audience for programmes of this kind generally represents only a minority in each country.

It does happen that a section of the public will, at least occasionally, watch a drama programme, or even a news programme, in a language which it does not fully understand if the images shown enable viewers to decode the sense of what is happening. But on the whole language represents a barrier which reduces the numbers of people who can actually be reached by programmes throughout Europe.

According to the survey undertaken for *PETAR* (Pan-European Television Audience Research), the pan-European channels which have had the greatest success in reaching an international audience at the present time are the English-language **Sky Channel** and **Super Channel**, which are reported to have reached respectively 20% and 7% of the audience in cabled homes in the Scandinavian countries, 6% and 2% in the Netherlands, 5% and 2% in Belgium-Luxemburg, 2% and 1% in the Federal Republic of Germany. The survey also confirms that Sky is particularly well regarded by young people, and that its success is especially marked in the Nordic countries which do not yet have national commercial services and where, as a result, competition for undemanding programmes is weakest.

The programmes transmitted by satellite to the various cable systems can now be provided with sub-titling which differs according to country, but this sub-titling can be most easily applied to pre-recorded programmes, such as films, and the limited effectiveness of sub-titling in a good many countries is already well known. Direct broadcast satellites will adopt a standard which will make it possible to use several sound-tracks in parallel; this technical advance will have a particularly beneficial effect in the case of pre-recorded programmes, as well as for reports — particularly those dealing with sports — in which journalists restrict themselves to commenting on images without actually appearing on the screen. The experiments carried out by **Europa tv** and referred to in Chapter 6 have already shown the complex problems involved in the simultaneous presentation of one programme in several languages, the difficulty of sub-titling live transmissions (especially current affairs programmes), the inadequacy of superimposed translations, the lack of any personality in the words spoken, when the voice which is heard is not that of the journalist who is speaking, the enormous cost and the considerable work needed to provide translations in several languages; and above all the difficulty of adapting the same message to fit different perceptions of viewers in the various European countries, which are so complex not only in linguistic, but also in cultural respects.

The transnational impact of programmes in the same language

The use of the same language does not solve all the problems of communication between countries. Programmes originating in the Netherlands appear to be watched more in Flanders than are Flemish programmes in the Netherlands. If this is the case, the reason is probably that the consideration given to a neighbour who speaks the same language is not the same on both sides of the frontier. In the French community of Belgium, programmes emanating from France have a prestige which anything from Paris, whether entertainment or culture, generally enjoys in French-speaking countries. Except in a few places which are cabled, programmes emanating from Belgium are received only in the frontier areas of France. It remains to be seen whether, if they were to reach Paris, they would be received other than with the degree of condescension with which programmes which come from Switzerland, Canada or merely from the French provinces are received.

This is a well known phenomenon which applies to every aspect of cultural life: the international circulation of ideas and works of art does not create the same reverberations in every direction. There are poles which exert a strong influence on what surrounds them, but which are only slightly influenced in their turn. For all their prestige and the great resources at the disposal of the French television organisations, programmes from France do not find particular favour with the French-speaking Belgian public, which prefers programmes produced in Belgium. This tendency is still more marked in Flanders, to the advantage of Flemish programmes, and in the Netherlands to that of Dutch programmes.

The public is especially fond of a daily news programme presented not only in its own language, but based on its own environment, and commented on and explained for its benefit by journalists who know the problems and concerns of that public. Of course, some viewers are happy to be able to get to know the news "as seen by others", but this concern is demonstrated only by small groups, and by an intellectual élite. This psychological reaction should not be ignored, since it will probably be one of the major obstacles to the success of a European news service, which the European Parliament and many people of good will are anxious to see established. It is not certain that for the development of a European consciousness, it is enough to say the same thing at the same time using television: one cannot speak of the problem of wine and butter to every European in the same way in every country of the Community. The explanations must be different, depending on the audience being addressed; otherwise, such explanations are unlikely to be either adequate or sufficiently interesting.

Hence, the obstacles to the creation of an effective European news service, as discussed in Chapter 6, capable of being transmitted across frontiers are not only linguistic. The progress of technology will not be enough to solve them. In competition, the programmes which stand up best appear to be the national or regional news programmes. Those which are least resistant to competition are cultural programmes: the great increase in entertainment programmes in the general climate of commercialisation is harmful to the more serious programmes, the minority audience for which is being noticeably reduced still further. The audience is being fragmented, but the relative share taken by entertainment programmes — and, among these, by drama programmes — is still growing. The programmes which travel most easily across frontiers — provided, of course, that the language used is understood by the viewer — are "ready-made" programmes such as films, serials and series.

So far as cinema films are concerned, the general-interest channels are threatened by pay-channels and by video. This development is already clear-cut in the United States

Table 2.4: Video recorder ownership in 1987
(as a percentage of television households)

Country	Percentage
A	19
B	21
CH	27
D	34
DK	31
E	27
F	32
GB	55
GR	19
I	11
IRL	43
L	25
N	35
NL	38
P	21
S	33
SF	31

Source: National sources, Screen Digest, MIP-COM 87, IFPI

where, to avoid the numerous breaks made necessary by advertising, many viewers are taking refuge in the specialist channels, which offer more recent films than the open channels, and show them repeatedly at different times of the day. In Europe, until now only **Canal Plus** in France has succeeded in being profitable as a pay-channel.

Video, used both to record television programmes and to show rented or purchased tapes, most commonly of cinema films, is expanding rapidly, but its development is very unequal, as is shown in Table 2.4. In 1987, 55% of homes in the United Kingdom were equipped with video-recorders; in Ireland the figure was 43%, 38% in the Netherlands, and 34% in the Federal Republic of Germany, but it was still only 32% in France, 27% in Spain, 21% in Belgium, 19% in Austria and 11% in Italy. The reason for this appears to be a difference in approach to the renting or hire-purchase of consumer durables. Between now and the end of the century, audiovisual technologies will expand still further, and video will probably do so more rapidly than the rest. The direct broadcast satellites − if receiving equipment and the decoding system can be made commercially available at relatively little cost − and medium-powered satellites of the *ASTRA* type, will be able to contribute a number of pan-European programmes to the overall scene; these will be received immediately in the cabled areas and will gradually reach other regions as well.

Experience up to now suggests that some of the more extravagant hopes which have been expressed are Utopian. The technology which makes it possible to increase considerably the number of programme services and to transmit them across frontiers does not guarantee that they will actually be watched by viewers. The linguistic and cultural barriers will not be easily dismantled, particularly in the field of news. The persistence of linguistic and cultural differences should reassure those who fear that television will become uniform and will destroy the cultural identity of the countries which make up Europe.

It is beyond dispute, however, that a substantial proportion of European television has come to be regarded by those who control it as an industry which is justified only if it reaps profits. There is already keen competition to conquer the more profitable areas of an expanding market. The European Television Task Force is afraid that, with such a spirit prevailing, the concern for the profitability of programmes may come to eclipse the concern for quality. It takes the view that new television stations are justified only if they satisfy certain criteria of quality; if they do not confine themselves to transmitting bought-in products, but contribute to the creation of television programmes which will reflect the specific characteristics of European culture.

The Task Force is convinced that not every type of programme can be made profitable through advertising, or by subscription systems or by piecemeal purchase. It is desirable, however, that at the European level as at the national level, in addition to general-interest programmes designed to entertain a mass audience, or thematic programmes based on the cinema, sport or popular music, there should be programmes which are deliberately aimed at minority audiences. It is important that programmes in the European languages should be available throughout Europe on specialist channels, even if in most countries they will be viewed by only limited audiences. It is important that programmes should be made which use and make apparent the riches of the European heritage in music, dance, the theatre the visual arts and literature. Programmes of quality deserve the support of public funds.

We discuss the nature of quality in television in Chapter 3. In Chapter 4 we go on to consider how a European framework could prevent the new television services from giving rise to anarchic competition in the audiovisual sphere. In Chapter 5 the Task Force discusses the need for a dynamic television industry which will guarantee a minimum degree of quality for European television. Our aim is to provide concrete proposals for action in each area.

Chapter 3
Quality in Television

The components of quality

It emerged at an early stage of discussion that the aim must be to find a framework for European television which would secure quality in all types of services, existing and new, public and private. That decision informed all subsequent work, which has concentrated on the central question of how to achieve quality in a diversified and pluralist European television system largely unfettered by traditional mechanisms of control.

There was no collective preconception in favour of public broadcasting systems compared with private ones. Good broadcasting can be achieved by both kinds of system and both should be allowed to play their proper roles in the emerging mixed economy of broadcasting.

The existing national services represent an essential, and continuing, feature in the European television landscape. But they are not entitled to stand still, however impressive past records may be. Tradition, pride in past achievements and established standards are all of importance, but they should be seen as incentives to further development. The existing services must continually aim to improve performance and to adapt their attitudes, policies and practices to what are now rapidly changing circumstances.

Private services, both existing and to come, must also aim at high standards in serving their audiences. Those standards will not necessarily be identical in all respects — particularly, for example, in the case of specialised services — with those which have applied so far.

Cultural diversity — an essential consideration

Before considering how to secure quality, it is necessary to explain what the term means. It does not denote, as is sometimes thought, "high culture". It has far wider meaning and a number of components, programme and technical.. It is a precondition of quality for the new mixed system of television which is emerging that the system, taken as a whole, should reflect and promote cultural diversity at all levels:

- at the level of Europe;

- at the national level;

- at that of the separate regions, minorities and language groups within countries.

Diversity is at present substantially provided by the general programmes of the national broadcasting organisations and by the regional services for such areas as Catalonia, Galicia, the Alto Adige, Friesland, the Basque country, Brittany, Flanders, Wallonia and Wales. It will be a test of new services to see the extent to which, in the long run, they make a real contribution to the cause of cultural diversity.

Diversity in the make-up of the programmes as a whole has to be demonstrated in the following ways:

- there must be diversity in programme content, with a proper balance being kept between the basic functions of television: information, education and entertainment;

- the identity, tastes and interests of the audience (regional, national or European) should be catered for;

- provision should be made for a diversity in programme making: more and more throughout Europe is the desirability being recognised of the use of independent producers to provide a proportion of programmes alongside in-house productions.

Original programming

A programme supply of quality is unlikely to consist predominantly of ready-made productions for it would not possess the necessary elements of diversity referred to above. It should contain also a significant proportion of original material produced, commissioned and/or financed by the providers of the service. This is of particular importance in circumstances where ready-made productions would be likely to consist mainly of programmes from the United States, for this would conflict with our wish to see programme services reflecting Europe's cultural diversity. But original programming has not only the relevance of avoiding imports from outside Europe. It has a more intrinsic importance for programme quality:

- it provides a continuity and distinctiveness of style in the same way as the best film, theatre, opera and ballet companies and the best newspapers have their own style which stamps an imprint of quality on them;

- it gives the opportunity for that style to be developed in the field of television where the ability to innovate and experiment is essential;

- it enables talent and creativity to be fostered.

General and specialised programmes

However, programme quality in its general aspects of diversity and breadth of material and a sufficient provision of originated programming should be judged across the whole range of the output receivable by the viewer from various services rather than by reference to the nature of any one service alone. The criterion, in a situation of multiple choice, is how far the totality of services available — general and specialised — adequately achieves the overall requirements. Thus specialised or thematic services can properly contribute to a range of services (receivable in the same place) which combine to provide a supply of quality programmes in the sense defined above. At the same time, we would expect to see all services striving in the long run to produce and promote the production of original European programme material and that this responsibility should not belong only to the public services.

News and current affairs programmes

News and current affairs programmes constitute an important element in quality broadcasting. In these categories, the output as a whole should be fair and balanced. But the components of a quality service go further than mere fairness, important as that is. It should be comprehensive in its coverage of national and international matters and in representing all significant strands of political and social opinion. It should strive for accuracy. Also, as well as gathering and presenting facts, it should set them in a proper context of analysis and explanation. All these requirements mean that news and current affairs programmes should attract a reasonable share of money and production resources.

Quality of individual programmes: the need for professionalism

We take it for granted that the aim of all good broadcasting should be that the individual items in the schedules are as good of their kind as they can be. This applies to all programmes, light and serious, for it is no part of our thinking that avowedly popular programmes are of lesser quality than those designed to appeal to minority or specialised tastes nor is quality exclusively dependent on the size of the programme budget. Some items may have quite modest aims and the resources available for them may be correspondingly limited. This is not necessarily a drawback, for simplicity and sincerity are aspects of quality. What is essential throughout the schedules is the professionalism of the creative and production staff and the willingness of those in control of television services to back that professionalism financially and in other ways.

Respect for creative work

A television service of quality is one which respects the integrity of the creative material which it uses. This should not be altered or treated in ways which are in conflict with the author's intention or reputation. This "moral right" of authors to receive due credit for their works and to have them properly respected is defined in Article 6bis of the Berne Convention. Those handling creative material should understand the purpose of that Article; to ensure that the right is generally observed, it is recommended that provisions reflecting the terms of the Article be included in the national legislation of all European countries.

Accountability to the public as an aspect of programme quality

Many existing broadcasting systems incorporate methods by which the services can be plainly seen to be accountable to the public. These aims may be achieved structurally by the creation of authorities and governing bodies which have the job of acting as trustees of the public interest and of seeing that the broadcasters comply with the requirements placed on them by their statutes or charters. Such structural provisions can be tailored to fit the particular social or cultural needs of a country. For example, we were impressed, when we visited the Netherlands, by the durability of the long-established system whereby various political, religious and cultural movements in Dutch society form an integral part of the programme provision arrangements and ensure accountability to the viewers.

Elsewhere, accountability provisions include the appointment of consultative and advisory bodies representative of the public at large, of particular interest groups or of groups of experts in various programme fields. Other elements of programme accountability are to be found in respect for the audience, through compliance with measures governing such basic matters as the provision of a right of reply, the avoidance of pornography, gratuitous violence or incitement to race hatred and standards for broadcast advertising, and in responsiveness to the audience's tastes and interests as demonstrated in research findings, particularly qualitative ones (for example in appreciation indices). In new private services it will be more difficult to incorporate elements of structural accountability, although they may be present to some extent. But they can do much to accept, and demonstrate their willingness to meet, the need to be responsive to the audiences for which they cater.

The achievement of programme quality

Quality is an aim to be achieved by positive and liberating measures although some regulatory measures also need to be enunciated and applied. The coming years, until the end of the century, should not be regarded as only presenting problems which require regulation to solve them: they also provide the chance to release creative resources which have not been able to find their full outlet in the more restrictive past. By using such resources to the full and by establishing a framework of civilised competition, the benefits of a greater genuine choice for European audiences can be achieved and the dangers of increased choice leading to a loss of quality overall can be much reduced.

The promotion of production in Europe to match the demand for more programmes (see the following paragraph) requires positive encouragement to all sectors of the audiovisual industry to undertake production and co-production and to improve programme distribution among all countries. In the case of the television organisations, such incentives should be open to all, private as well as public. In fact, such opportunities may well prove to be more important to the newly emerging services, at least in their early years, in encouraging the production of new programmes for them to broadcast in preference to existing material.

The demand for increased production

Europe has before it the prospect — indeed the necessity — of increasing its audiovisual production. At present Western European broadcasters transmit some 150 000 hours of television each year, of which they produce or commission about 100 000 hours. The remaining 50 000 hours consist of bought-in programmes, 20 000 hours coming from the United States. An EC report said in 1983 that, with coming developments and new services, the requirement of originated television and cinema material would rise to perhaps 500 000 hours a year — about five times the present figure. It now seems clear that this figure is too high. Even so, there can be no doubt that there is a large and growing demand for programme material. The extent to which that demand can be filled by new European audiovisual production and how much will be bought in, largely from the United States, remains to be seen and must depend to a significant extent on the availability and effectiveness of special promotional measures to encourage production and to secure effective distribution of new programmes. Success in increasing Europe's own production capacity will be a significant factor in preserving quality in its television output.

Technical quality

If viewers are to have quality of technical reception to match the programme quality which should be the aim for the future, then the technical standards of production and transmission in all services should meet the generally applicable requirements. This report assumes throughout its discussion of the possible developments of television that these standards will be observed. They originate from the International Telecommunication Union and its committees which lay down the international standards for the technical equipment used for production, post-production, distribution and broadcasting of television programmes. In this context it will be important for a universally acceptable decision to be reached in Europe about the exact MAC standard which should be used for DBS transmissions and which would suit modern cable systems. Without this, the higher quality of transmission will not be universally available at reasonable cost and future moves to high definition television will be prejudiced. These matters have been dealt with in detail in Chapter 2.

The importance of finance for quality

It has become clear, particularly from our hearings with broadcasters of all kinds from many parts of Europe, that the achievement of quality cannot be separated from the availability of money. This is as true of technical quality as it is of programmes. An injection of cash will not automatically convert a poor service into a good one; but it is unlikely that a service which is inadequately funded for the aims which it has set itself, or which have been prescribed for it, will be able to provide a service of quality. It is for this reason that we have given close attention to broadcasting finance in the final section of this chapter.

Advertising and quality

The classic model of European public service television is one in which broadcasting organisations have relied exclusively on licence fees paid by the viewers for their income. As costs have increased and the potential role of television as an advertising medium has become appreciated, public service television services BEGAN more and more to look to advertising revenue to contribute a proportion of their income. The proportion of the total income of individual television organisations which this represents is shown in Table 3.1..

Advertising transmitted by the public service broadcasters has been subject to strict control mechanisms imposed by governments, or by quasi-governmental organisations appointed for this purpose, or by the broadcasters themselves as part of their public accountability. The strictest controls are those imposed by the Swiss Government on advertising transmitted by the Swiss Broadcasting Corporation.[1] The Code of Advertising Conduct applied to advertising by the Independent Broadcasting Authority of the United Kingdom under obligations imposed on it by Acts of

---

1   For details see "Die SRG im Gesellschaftlichen Umfeld", Bern, SRG, 1987 p. 60.

Parliament is generally regarded as the most detailed and extensive statement of the requirement of the public interest in regard to television advertising.[1]

As private enterprise in television has come to be encouraged by a number of European governments, there is strong pressure from the advertising industry (advertisers and agencies) both for more television advertising time and for access to the new television services. The European Advertising Tripartite, giving evidence to the Task Force, reiterated its 1986 statement that:

"Advertisers need more television in Europe; and multi-market advertisers need the option of multi-market media to carry uniform commercial messages when these are considered to be the most appropriate cost-effective way to reach and move their target markets"[2]

A possible increase in the volume of advertising on television calls for careful thought in relation to the general quality of the output. For example, Article 14 of the latest draft of the European Commission's Directive on Broadcasting lays down a daily limit of 15% of broadcasting time for advertisements , and an hourly limit of 18% in cross-frontier transmissions within the Community. The draft Council of Europe Convention proposes an overall limit of 15% for normal spot advertising.[3] These percentages are higher than existing maxima in most European national advertising regulations. Although, realistically, it may be necessary to accept them for new trans-frontier services, there is some reason to fear that, if these percentages are agreed for such services, there will be pressure from the advertising industry to move towards higher percentages for national television services. Whether advertisers succeed in such moves depends on national authorities' decisions.

More significantly, some governments would like to shift the balance of funding for television services from public sources towards advertising as a source of revenue. This has already happened in France and was considered by the United Kingdom Government until advised to the contrary by the Peacock Committee. In the Federal Republic of Germany public service broadcasters are, without direct pressure from

1   "The IBA Code of Advertising Standards and Practices", London, IBA Reprinted July 1986
2   EAAA 1986
3   For a fuller discussion of EC and Council of Europe proposals for legislation see Chapter 4.

Table 3.1: Advertising revenue as a percentage of total income of European public service broadcasters

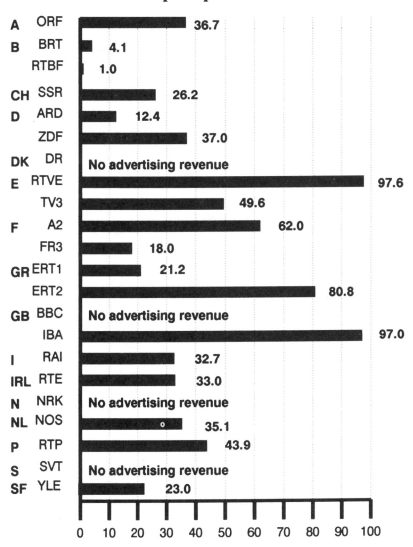

Source: European Institute for the Media/EBU 1985/1986

49

the Government, having to increase their reliance on advertising revenue due to rising costs coupled with static licence revenue.[1]

All these trends and pressures for increased advertising time and increased dependence on advertising carry the danger of there being a major distortion of the function of television itself, in which it can easily become merely a weapon in the marketing strategy of manufacturers of goods and services, with programmes designed primarily to attract and retain an audience for advertisers. Other viewer concerns about the future of television advertising focus on shifting boundaries in relation to the timing and grouping of advertisements, to the differing national lists of goods and services whose advertising is prohibited and to the need for the content of advertising to be checked before transmission.

The Task Force has identified the following ways in which advertising, if uncontrolled, can affect the quality of television services:

- overemphasis on the advertising role could turn television services essentially into vehicles for advertising: programme content is then relevant only in so far as it attracts viewers who can be exposed to advertising;

- even if such prime commercial motivation is absent, excessive advertising can detract from the value of television as a medium for information, education, culture and entertainment;

- it may be distributed, in terms of its frequency and of the way in which it is inserted, so as to detract from the integrity of the programme material: in extreme cases, it may be deliberately included in the programmes so as to blur the essential distinction between what is programme content and what is advertising;

- methods of advertising may be harmful by, for example, being misleading, appealing to fear or abusing the credulity of children;

- the subject-matter of the advertising may be undesirable, for example, cigarettes or certain medical claims.

1   See "Media Bulletin", Manchester, European Institute for the Media, 1987, Vol.4 No.4, page 8.

So far, as has been said above, such matters have, with varying degrees of effectiveness, been dealt with by national governments and authorities, and advertisers themselves have exercised a measure of self-regulation.

With the growing number of transfrontier services and the increasing commercialisation of television, it will be important, as is suggested in Chapter 1, to have standard rules for transfrontier services. Chapter 4 describes the activities of the European Commission and the Council of Europe in this area. For our part, we consider that the minimum regulations applicable throughout Europe should cover the following aspects:

● advertising must be entirely separate and distinct from the programmes;

● advertising should not be so excessive in amount that it detracts from the quality of the programme service;

● advertising should be distributed so as to avoid breaching the integrity and value of individual programmes and so as to cause a minimum disruption for the viewers;

● advertising should be of high standard as regards its content and its method of presentation, and adequate arrangements for considering in advance its content and presentation should be established.

We are aware that, at the present time, discussions are continuing in Europe about the allowable ways in which advertising should be inserted into programme services and whether this should be allowed only between programmes or whether interruption of programmes in "natural breaks" is to be permissible. The difference of opinion in this field stems from the two traditions of placing advertising in fairly long "blocks" or putting it in more frequent, but shorter, advertising intervals, including ones within programmes. We consider that it should be possible to reach a solution which does not oblige broadcasters to operate, if they do not wish to do so, in one particular way. The prime aim must be to serve the viewers' interest, while accepting that television services must earn enough revenue to provide good programmes (including a due proportion of original material). Advertising in blocks, in a far more competitive world, may well not achieve this, particularly as new technology enables viewers to "zap", either by using the remote control to switch channels when advertisements come on, or by pressing the fast-forward to skip the commercials when playing back programmes on a video recorder.

Sponsorship

The demands of advertisers for more time on television and for new ways of communicating their message have converged with broadcasting organisations' financial needs to cause them both to see sponsorship in an increasingly attractive light. The term sponsorship covers a wide variety of financial arrangements between broadcasting organisations, programme providers and outside commercial enterprises. It is useful to maintain the operational distinction between the televising of commercially sponsored events, which the broadcasters regard as of interest to their viewers, for example, a major golf tournament on the one hand, and commercially sponsored programmes on the other.

The attitude of viewers to sponsorship was tested in 1984 by the National Consumer Council of the United Kingdom. The survey did not reveal overwhelming consumer opposition to the sponsorship of programmes on cable television. It did, however, show evidence of discrimination by viewers between the types of programmes which they regarded as suitable for sponsorship. While a majority favoured sponsorship of sport, music, quiz and comedy programmes, there was a majority against sponsorship of news and current affairs. There was also a strong objection to any influence being exercised by sponsors on programme content: nearly four in five consumers were against sponsors having complete control of programmes, while two in three were against sponsors having any influence over programme content.

In our view the right approach to sponsorship bearing in mind the interests of the viewer, is based on the principles that:

- in all television programmes, whether distributed terrestrially, by satellite or by cable, sponsored material should be clearly distinguishable so that viewers are in no doubt about what is being provided from sponsors and what comes on the sole responsibility of the service provider;

- sponsors should not supply or influence editorial material i.e. that which is provided by the broadcaster.

Even if these two principles are accepted, much remains to be done to work out a European code to govern sponsorship and to ensure that it is observed.

Finance and quality

Adequate funding is an essential element in securing programme and technical quality. It is particularly so in the case of new services. An established service which becomes squeezed for income has at least the advantage of not having to find start-up costs and of not having to build up from nothing an audience large enough to amortise those costs and to meet running expenses. Virtually all the new services being developed now and in the future face a central difficulty in obtaining viewers: unlike terrestrial services in the past, they have, before they can attract viewers away from other services, to persuade them, or their cable suppliers, to equip themselves with the technical means of reception. Without an audience, they cannot earn income, whether from advertising or from subscription.

Sources of income

Licence fees

Licence revenue is the traditional way by which national public service broadcasting systems are financed. Independent Television (**ITV**) and **Channel Four**, the two arms of the United Kingdom Independent Broadcasting Authority's television service, and **RTVE** (Radio Televisione Española) of Spain, represent the only public systems of television in large European countries which are wholly self-supporting from advertising).

The licence fee remains a matter for national fixing and collection. The main issues raised in relation to the Task Force's remit concern the impact on licence fee supported national services of new competitive transfrontier operations. In particular, we would stress the following points:

● If competition grows substantially in any given country, the size of the licence fee will to a very large extent determine the ability of the national services to maintain quality in their sector of broadcasting. A drop in their audience share as a result of competition is not in itself a good reason for not keeping the licence fee at a proper level. This would lead to a downward spiral, with quality (and therefore audience appeal) falling in line with reducing income.

- Broadcasting organisations receiving licence fee income must for their part, and in their own long-term interests, be able to demonstrate convincingly that, while fully discharging their programme obligations, they are both efficient and ready to adapt to the new broadcasting environment. Such demonstration will call for a readiness for the organisations concerned to be open about the details of their expenditure and to be willing to undergo periodically some efficiency audit.

- Competition tends to lead to an increase in programme costs. Those who fix the licence fee must take this into account when they periodically carry out a review. We note from Table 3.2 that some licence fees are currently significantly lower than others; it will plainly be easier for some of the countries concerned to adjust fees upwards, if necessary, than others, although we accept that the economic position of particular countries must be taken into account.

- Licence fees should not be reduced in pursuance of a policy that public services should be deliberately restricted in programme range and should concentrate on the more serious and thoughtful categories.

- A large part of Europe's programme production, both television and film, depends at this stage upon the health of the licence-supported broadcasters, as does the European and national character of the programmes as a whole. The new services must be encouraged to play their own part, when they are able to do so, in accepting similar responsibilities.

The point came up in our discussions with broadcasters whether, to enable private services to develop and prosper, those public services which are dependent upon mixed licence fee and advertising revenue, should cease to take advertising and rely solely on licences. As can be seen from Table 3.1, advertising revenue is so significant a factor in the financing of existing national services that we cannot regard this idea as desirable or realistic.

Government grants

Financing of broadcasting services by direct government grant or by specific taxation is not favoured in Western Europe. The overriding reason, with which we agree, is that direct financing of this kind must jeopardise the continuing independence of the broadcasters. However, if, for industrial rather than broadcasting reasons, Government assistance is given, as it has been in France and Germany, for instance, to the development and putting into service of satellite broadcasting transmission equipment, we would see no objection, indeed, we would consider it as a desirable impetus to the technical facilities essential to the changing television landscape. But we do suggest that governments should not take decisions to support new technology in this way in isolation from their overall broadcasting policies. For example, an understandable desire to promote a country's electronic or aerospace industry may have significant implications for existing terrestrial services and those taking the industrial decisions should be aware of such implications. Again, industrial moves facilitating the introduction of new services must be related to coherent policies about the standards expected of such services and about the means of securing their observance.

Advertising

Table 3.1 shows the importance of advertising revenue in the general financing of Europe's national broadcasting services. Table 2.1, which describes the new low-power satellite services, confirms its continuing importance in the new era of broadcasting. From the point of view of the Task Force's terms of reference, the main specifically financial point concerning advertising has been the extent to which competition from new services is likely to affect the ability of existing terrestrial services to continue to discharge their established programme obligations.

Our broad answer (and we cannot be more precise) is: there will be an effect but it will not be uniform in timing or weight across all countries. For example, in our discussion in the United Kingdom with the Independent Broadcasting Authority we gained the clear impression that they were not concerned for the foreseeable future about the ability of their two television services, totally dependent upon advertising, to withstand competition from satellite-delivered services. In other countries, transfrontier competition for advertising, mainly from the CLT and its associated companies, has existed for some while. The systems exposed to it seem to have adapted to it and should be able to weather some additional fragmentation of the audience. These views find some confirmation in, the European Institute for the Media's study *Media in Competition*[1] This study suggests that the erosion of the monopoly or nearmonopoly of national network television services, which has already begun, will proceed much less rapidly than forecast by the developers of competitive new ser-

1   ". Media in Competition": The European Institute for the Media and InterMedia Centrum
      Hamburg. Manchester and Hamburg 1986

Table 3.2:
European television licence fees in 1988, in ecu

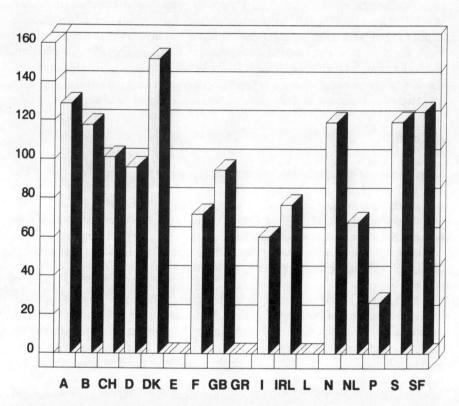

Notes:

1: There is no licence fee in Luxemburg or Spain.. In Greece television set-owners are charged an additional sum on the domestic electricity bill.

2: The Table shows the licence fee payable for a domesticcolour receiver. In some countries differential rates are applied to hotels and other public places, and separate fees are charged for radio. These rates are not shown.

Source: National sources, compiled by the European Institute for the Media

vices and will not lead to a fundamental change in the pattern of national television services during the next decade. The study, however, does sound a note of warning about the progressive erosion from within, over the next fifteen years or so, of such services, particularly in the smaller countries, as the gaps between production costs and revenues widen.

Even if our own views are too sanguine, it must be for each country to decide for itself how far it wants to protect and support existing services and how it should do so. There can be no uniform answer. In the United Kingdom, for instance, there have been preliminary suggestions that, since two out of the four national public services are self-supporting — and therefore most vulnerable to competition — they should, if the need emerges, receive some licence fee support. It is not for us to comment on this suggestion beyond noting it as the kind of decision which all countries may, in due course, need to consider.

Sponsorship

Advertising interests put forward the view that sponsorship is not really advertising but is rather a form of patronage or a particular way of financing programmes. The UK Committee on Financing the BBC (The Peacock Committee) defined sponsorship as "a form of advertising limited to a statement in a particular programme that it is being financed by a particular organisation", with other intrusive advertising being normally excluded. We have dealt with some of the policy aspects of sponsorship earlier in this chapter. It is necessary only to say here that sponsorship is a supplementary source of funds which would in many cases come, at least in part, out of television advertising appropriations.

Subscription (including pay-per-programme)

Under a system of subscription television, the viewers, instead of receiving programmes without further charge (as with programmes financed from licence revenue or by advertising), choose and pay for what they view. This choice and payment may be related to tiers of services (the basic and premium tiers of some existing cable operations), or to whole programme services, or even to individual programme items (pay-per-programme). Although there is nothing in principle, nor any technical reason, against advertising being included in subscription or pay-per-programme television services, one of the advantages seen for this type of provision is that it enables programmes to be supplied which are clear of advertising or which contain less advertising than would otherwise be the case.

Another feature of subscription television is that the programmes tend to be of a particular "premium" kind: i.e. some high quality additions to what is provided by the generally available television services. The reasons for this are not far to seek: firstly, people are likely to be most willing to pay extra for something special which is available only to them; secondly, programme suppliers, particularly of current films, prefer the box office characteristics of subscription television where they are paid, directly or indirectly, according to a programme's appeal to the audience and where the limited exposure does not, in the case of a film, spoil entirely the income to be received from theatrical distribution and, in the case of other programmes, does not rule out the chance of later showing it generally on open access television.

As a Task Force we are particularly interested in the income potential of transfrontier subscription television and the extent to which it will support a worthwhile standard of programming and a good level of originated programmes. The European evidence of likely demand is slender. The most successful subscription service is **Canal Plus** in France. This now covers 2.2 million subscribers, a figure reached in three years and one which accounts for by far the largest part of the total of European pay television subscribers. The Canal Plus encrypted signal is available to 12 per cent of all French television homes. The monthly cost of subscription is 23 ecu. In the United States, some 27 million homes (31 per cent of the total of US television homes), using a variety of reception methods, predominantly cable, are pay television subscribers. This figure has been reached over a period of some fifteen years. The cost per channel averages out at about 10 ecu a month.

Europe is different from the United States in having on offer virtually everywhere varied and popular national services. It is also less widely cabled than is the United States. All the same, it is clear that even a relatively low penetration of subscription services, whether available from satellite or via cable, could produce substantial revenue which could feed into the European audiovisual industry (although, no doubt, many premium films would be of US origin). Thus an eventual 10 per cent take-up, giving 12 million European homes, at a relatively low average subscription level of 15 ecu per month (180 ecu per annum), would produce an annual subscription income of more than two thousand million ecu, which is about one-fifth of the current annual revenue of Europe's television services from all sources. However, take-up of subscription services is likely to be very variable in the different countries, and while ten percent may not seem a very high proportion, it may be some time before it becomes the average penetration across Europe as a whole.

Financing of new services by levies on other services

Channel Four in the United Kingdom is an example (the only one so far) of a new service being financed out of the income earned by other services. Such a system of raising money to finance a television service must grow out of national circumstances and needs and can have no universal application. But the desirability of some central funds for assistance to European production activities leads us to suggest in Chapter 5 that a central support fund for audiovisual production could be raised by a levy on the turnover of all members of the audiovisual industry, (See Recommendation 5.8)

Increased costs for international rights

Transfrontier broadcasting requires the acquisition of international rights in programme material and the negotiation of international arrangements with artists and others concerned in the making of programmes. These will almost certainly lead to increased costs, compared with national programmes, even though the international audience may in practice be no greater than what it would be for a corresponding national programme.

Language transfer

Another additional cost element in transfrontier programming is that of securing intelligibility to an international audience. As examples, the average cost of subtitling an hour of completed programming is 740 ecu, of dubbing is 11 000 ecu, of voice-over 1 500 ecu and of narration 1 100 ecu. The average hourly production cost of a programme for international transmission in Europe is about 85 000 ecu. While the costs of sub-titling and voice over would not seem excessive, particularly if only one or two languages were involved, full dubbing, even for one sound channel only, would be a significant additional expense if it were done regularly, as in the case of France, the Federal Republic of Germany, and Italy [1].

---

1   see also: The European Institute for the Media: Overcoming Language Barriers in European
    Television, forthcoming (Autumn 1988)

Concluding remarks

The future television landscape, as has already been explained, will be far more competitive than hitherto and will lead, sooner or later, to audience fragmentation. These factors will make securing quality more difficult for all services than it has been in the past, when, in the main, national services have operated in a protected environment. Past experience has shown that competition can lead to improvements in the service provided to the viewing public. These can come not only from an increase in choice and in diversity of programme provision but also from a sharpening of the performance on the part of established services. But such improvements are likely only to reduce, and not to remove entirely, the problems which can arise over quality. In particular, it will be necessary to secure:

- a minimum framework of international regulation to secure that competition among all services — public and private, new and existing — is on a fair footing;

- a stable and prosperous European production industry, through adequately financed television services and through positive measures of support.

In these ways a European cultural identity will be achieved in the total television output and the dangers of economic decline can be avoided. Chapters 4 and 5 respectively develop both these matters.

Chapter 4
A European framework for competition

The development of television in Europe has often been regarded as consisting of a keen and unavoidable conflict between public service organisations and private companies operating on a commercial basis. In fact, owing to dramatic changes in technology as well as to the liberalising media policies which have been adopted for some years now in most countries, the public service monopoly has ceased to exist virtually everywhere. The problem to be tackled in the future is to see whether a harmonious system can emerge, based on a set of minimum rules which would ensure peaceful coexistence — and perhaps cooperation — between the public service and the commercial broadcasting organisations, with the aim of expanding the audiovisual sphere in Europe.

The end of the public service monopoly has often been considered as forming part of the process of total deregulation. In fact, only in a few countries is this change taking place on a strict laissez-faire basis. Some countries, even those which are pursuing a more emphatic liberal policy, such as Great Britain, have for many years past applied standards which govern both public service and commercial organisations alike. Other countries, such as France, which authorised commercial television channels only a short time ago, have taken care to impose certain obligations on them. The concern to avoid total deregulation is therefore quite widespread.

The obligations of broadcasting organisations, public and private

It is now recognised that the concept of public service broadcasting does not depend on any specific legal instrument creating a relationship, direct or indirect, between a broadcasting organisation and the state. As was pointed out at the European Ministerial Conference on European Communications Policy (Vienna, December 1986), public service broadcasting principles can be observed by private as by public bodies. The determining factor is the obligation which the law imposes on the broadcasting organisation, or the regulations to which it is subject, or the obligations which it imposes on itself. It is generally recognised that these obligations must take into account the following objectives, which were also stated in the preparatory papers for the Vienna Conference:

● to provide a service accessible to all;

● to present news and current affairs objectively and independently of the state, and of other centres of power or interest groups;

● to safeguard freedom of expression by reflecting varied views and ideas, as well as a wide range of subjects;

● to promote national culture;

● to transmit programmes aimed at minority groups.

The European Broadcasting Union requires that a public broadcasting service should "undertake to provide in a community, for the general public, a varied, balanced blend of programmes, intended for all categories of the population, including minorities", that it should "be responsible for a significant proportion of the original output which it transmits, and should, in any case, have complete control of it", that it should "serve the public using the most appropriate technical means" and that it should "reinvest the major part of the profits from its activities in the development of broadcasting".

Public service broadcasting organisations cannot be defined only by their sources of finance; most are financed first and foremost by licence-fees and subsidies, but they often also rely on income from sponsorship and commercial advertising (see tab. 3.1 and 3.2). As far as the commercial television channels are concerned, their resources normally derive from advertising or from sponsorship. It is normal for them to want to achieve a satisfactory level of profitability from their activities.

But every form of broadcasting also carries with it social and cultural responsibilities. The use of terrestrial broadcasting frequencies, cable or satellite channels, generally derives from a licence granted by government. It is therefore a privilege which entails the observance of certain conditions in the public interest. Often the licence is subject to a number of conditions relating particularly to the content of the programmes transmitted. These conditions may be less restrictive in the case of private broadcasters than the obligations imposed on the public services. They must, however, have some moral basis and set standards of quality, as well as providing the basis for harmonious competition between all those concerned.

Advertising and sponsorship

As far as advertising is concerned, restrictions on certain products (such as tobacco and alcohol) are usually exactly the same for commercial as for public broadcasters. Differences can be seen in the duration of advertisements, and in the time at which they are transmitted, as well as in the possibility or impossibility of interrupting programmes (especially films). The laws and regulations are in some countries more flexible in the case of the commercial sector than in that of the public sector. Their aim is to establish a balance of resources between the commercial organisations which rely entirely on advertising, and the organisations which also receive income from licence-fees or subventions. Hence, an upper limit is often fixed for the advertising receipts which can accrue to public television services. In a number of countries – the United Kingdom and Belgium, for example – the public organisations are forbidden altogether to carry commercial advertising.

Commercial broadcasting organisations are keen to establish a clear division of resources: licence-fees and subsidies on the one hand, advertising on the other. As indicated in Chapter 3 (Recommendation 3.3) the European Television Task Force takes the view, that the public service should be guaranteed sufficient resources to carry out the full range of its functions. Advertising may be a secondary source of revenue to this end but it should be kept within the limits set out in the proposed Directive of the European Community (see page 69 below).

Individual rights, violence and decency

So far as obeying the law respecting the individual and the fundamental rights of others and standards with regard to violence and decency are concerned, the same requirements apply of course to the public and the commercial broadcasters.

News programmes

As far as news is concerned, commercial organisations, to the extent that they produce programmes of this kind at all, are generally required to conform to the same code of conduct as the public services in presenting news impartially and in reflecting different points of view. Their obligation to transmit programmes either made by governments, to transmit party political and trade union broadcasts, or to follow election campaigns varies according to the extent to which they are regarded as providing a public service.

Films and cultural programmes

With regard to the scheduling of films, similar provisions usually apply to commercial and to public organisations. These provisions lay down by law, regulations or agreements on the interval which must elapse before a film can be transmitted on television after it has been released for the cinema and the maximum number of films which can be shown on television. These provisions may also lay down, in greater or lesser detail, quotas for films of national or European origin.

So far as cultural programmes are concerned, commercial broadcasting organisations are not subject to the requirements which apply to the public broadcasters. They tend therefore to give priority to entertainment programmes. But the Task Force believes that it is undesirable to have a functional separation which would require the public services to restrict themselves to the field of culture and news and to leave entertainment to the commercial companies. Indeed, only by also providing entertainment can the public service retain a large enough audience to carry out effectively its obligations to provide information and culture.

Origination of programmes

In many countries broadcasters are obliged to produce themselves, or to commission from others, the production of original programmes. Such obligations are either implicit or formally required by quotas which are fixed either in hours of programmes to be transmitted or in terms of financial expenditure.

It is apparent that, in many countries where commercial broadcasting organisations have been allowed to operate, minimum regulations are imposed, especially with regard to the use of advertising, films, the standards of news presentation, programme content, and the production of original programmes. A degree of harmonisation thus tends to become established between the public and commercial organisations. We believe that this development is to be welcomed and that a coherent framework for the audiovisual sphere as a whole should be created, not only in every country but with respect to transfrontier broadcasting at the European level.

The role of the European Broadcasting Union

It is desirable that harmonisation among broadcasters at the international level should be undertaken at the professional level in the first place. The European Broadcasting Union, which has had a major role in the organisation of television, can play an important part in this respect. Founded in 1950 — at which time it took over from the International Broadcasting Union (IBU) — it is "a professional association of broadcasting organisations whose aim is to promote cooperation between its members and with broadcasting organisations throughout the world, and to represent the interests of its members in the programming, legal, technical and other fields". The EBU brings together as active members the organisations or groups of organisations in broadcasting which provide within the European broadcasting area as defined by the ITU "a broadcasting service of national character and national importance". By the statutes which were in force until February 1988, organisations wishing to be accepted as members had to guarantee to behave in a generally responsible manner, to provide a wide range of programmes (a substantial proportion of which they were to produce themselves), or had to be using, on a permanent basis, technical, broadcasting or transmission equipment for broadcasting services. In practice, this means that the EBU brings together the broadcasting organisations which have long occupied in each country a monopolistic or oligopolistic position, and these organisations have been joined in the last few years by several new bodies which conform to the stipulations laid down in the statutes. In the nature of things, most of the Union's members are public service organisations, but there have always been a few commercial organisations, such as RTL, among them.

Functions

The EBU is known particularly for programme exchanges, and for the arrangements which it has established among its members for news exchanges, especially as a result of the creation of the Eurovision network and of its permanent connections with sister Unions in other continents. The EBU provides technical services for its members to organise a terrestrial and satellite television network, to undertake research and to establish standards in every area of technology. At the legal level, it negotiates agreements with all the international professional interest groups (copyright, reproduction rights, the rights of music publishers, cable distributors, satellite operators, etc.); it represents the interests of its members in relation to international organisations, such as the European Commission and the Council of Europe; and it also negotiates world-wide contracts for major sporting events such as the Olympic Games, World Championship Football, etc.

Until recently this task could be carried out smoothly and to general satisfaction because television had grown up in a national context which determined the contributions which each member made (worked out on the basis of the number of viewers in each country). The benefits they received were worked out on an equitable basis for each country and, where oligopolies were involved, the distribution took place informally between the national members. The increase in the number of broadcasting organisations in many countries and the development of transnational operators mean that the task of the EBU is now a much more delicate one. The EBU has established rules which determine which rights shall have priority and the contributions which each member has to pay when programmes are broadcast transnationally.

Membership

For some years now the EBU has been debating whether this is the time to admit new categories of members. Among the new broadcasters, some are already playing a major role in their own countries, but have not yet been legally authorised (this is the case with the FININVEST networks in Italy). Others do not cover the whole country either by choice (as is the case with regional television stations in Spain) or in fact (as happens with **SAT 1** in Germany). Others again specialise in particular kinds of programme and do not provide the varied schedules required by the EBU's statutes. Others are merely transmitters of programmes and produce little of their own. Others, finally, have a transnational purpose without providing national coverage (this is the case with **Sky Channel**).

Without it being stated clearly, opposition to the admission to the Union of new members who satisfy only one or other of these criteria is, in some cases, motivated by fear of the competition which these new members would offer to existing members in acquiring the right to use the news networks and the right to show sporting events. On the supposition that membership became open to a wide range of broadcasters, the existing members — who represent the public service view of broadcasting — would also be in danger of becoming a minority in a Union dominated by a new type of operator. But if the latter are excluded from membership, there is a danger that the new television services might form a rival association to the EBU. In this way, mutually hostile blocs would be formed, which might try to outbid each other — to acquire, for example, the rights to sports programmes. This would damage everyone's interests, and in particular those of the television viewers.

New statutes

In February 1988, the EBU undertook the revision of its statutes, and this has led it to become relatively more open. The use of over the air broadcasting by ground-based transmitters is no longer the only criterion which must be met for a broadcasting service to be recognised by the Union; other broadcasting or transmission techniques have been approved: cable distribution systems, direct broadcast satellites and distribution by low-power satellites. But active members are still under an obligation to "cover the entire national population", and to guarantee that they really will provide "varied and balanced programming for all sections of the population, including a fair share of programmes catering for special minority interests of various sections of the public irrespective of the ratio of programme cost to audience". Further they should "actually produce and/or commission under their own editorial control a substantial proportion of the programmes broadcast" and they must, finally, "contribute actively to the radio and television programme exchanges and other EBU activities". These requirements make the earlier statutory requirements more precise, but do not in any way make them less rigorous.

The greater accessibility of the EBU can be seen in the fact that it may now accept as an active member "a group of broadcasting organisations" made up of "broadcasting organisations which individually, or, as regional organisations collectively, qualify for EBU membership". The grouping may also include "broadcasting organisations which provide specialised programme services in coordination with, and complementary to, the other group members' services" (which excludes the specialised independent rival services of the other members). Finally "consortia consisting exclusively of active members from different countries providing together a transnational television programme" may be recognised from now on as "Eurovision members".

Except for these cases, transnational television services cannot be accepted either as active members or as members of Eurovision. They can, however, obtain specific services from the Union, such as the use of the Eurovision network and the exchange of news by signing a contract and making payment.

The EBU may be right to maintain a cautious attitude towards new applications for membership and to want to have as members only organisations which satisfy the traditional aims and working methods which have prevailed so far in Europe. But, in these circumstances the EBU can no longer lay claim to be the body which regulates and coordinates the activities of all the broadcasting organisations operating in Europe.

The proposed Directive of the Commission of the European Communities on broadcasting across frontiers

The European countries have the sovereign right to regulate how television organisations which they have authorised should operate at a national level. In the age of transnational television the various states can no longer control the manner in which transfrontier services operating outside their borders operate. If the free circulation of programmes is to be encouraged and the development of television as a whole is to be safeguarded, a minimum number of international regulations must, therefore, be agreed upon.

The establishment of these minimum rules is the aim which the European Commission sets out in its proposed Directive on Broadcasting across Frontiers. This proposal was first published on 30 April 1986, and then modified considerably on 21 March 1988,[1] to take account of most of the amendments proposed in January of that year by the European Parliament. These amendments were made in response to a number of criticisms from various sources, and took up suggestions made by the European Institute for the Media[2]. They have unquestionably resulted in an improvement of the original texts.

The aim of the Directive is to apply Articles 55 and 62 of the Treaty of Rome to the field of broadcasting, that is to prohibit any restrictions on the free movement of the television programmes between the twelve Member States of the Community, and to implement Article 57 which provides for the coordination of national regulations, in order to make this freedom of movement a practical reality.

1   Amended proposal for a Council Directive on the co-ordination of certain provisions laid down by law, regulation or administrative action in Member States concerning the pursuit of broadcasting activities COM (88) 154 final 21/3/88
2   Cf. "Towards a European Market for Television: Contribution to the Debate "The European Institute for the Media, Media Monograph No. 8, Manchester, 1987

To this end, the Directive will contain a limited number of rules which, in various fields, will finally bring closer together the laws in force in various countries. Member States will not be able to object to programmes from other Member States being received and retransmitted on their own territory, provided that these programmes conform to the Directive.

General provisions and advertising

The harmonisation of programme content is limited to provisions relating to the protection of children and young people. It is interesting to note that the latest version of the proposed Directive requires every broadcasting organisation to provide a right of reply. The provisions relating to advertising constitute a code of professional conduct which is welcome. The provisions lay down, in particular, a maximum daily percentage of air time (15%) and of time per programme hour (18%) for advertising breaks. When the original draft Directive was being worked out, these figures were regarded by some as being too high in comparison with the limits imposed on the public broadcasting services; today, in the light of experience of the excesses which some countries have tolerated on the part of the new commercial broadcasters, they seem quite reasonable. It remains, however, a matter for regret for some that the Directive has abandoned its requirement that advertisements should be grouped together, and demands only that advertising should be "made quite distinct from the rest of the programme". The proposed Directive, taking account of the practical developments in the field of sponsorship, explicitly allows for this form of broadcasting finance but forbids any outside influence over the sponsored programme.

The question of copyright

The provisions dealing with copyright which initially formed part of the proposed Directive gave rise to fierce opposition from rights holders. They provided that, if no agreements were signed within two years between the copyright holder and a cable-distributors, the country concerned would ensure that a system of legal licensing was applied. In the current version of the proposal the principle of a compulsory licence is not formally abandoned, but, at the suggestion of the European Parliament, it will be applied only when other conciliation procedures have been exhausted. The member states will be obliged to encourage negotiations between the organisations which collectively manage copyright and neighbouring rights on the one hand, and the cable-distributors on the other. To resolve any disputes which may arise, member states will have to establish an arbitration tribunal on which there will be adequate representation for those who are entitled to the copyright and neighbouring rights. It is this arbitration body which will determine what is "equitable remuneration" for the acquisition of the rights at issue. It should be noted that the notion of "neighbouring rights" has been added to that of copyright, and that this will require the laws in the Community on such matters to be harmonised. Such legislation will also have to take explicitly into account all the means whereby programmes can be further exploited as a result of technical advances in the audiovisual field (recording, cable, various types of satellite, etc.).

The provision for arbitration will also have to apply to the broadcasting organisations (by amending in certain countries, if need be, the European agreement relating to the transfrontier transmission of programmes). The Task Force believes, however, that consideration should be given to the question of organisations which could well find it very difficult to operate if their programmes were transmitted across frontiers, and which would therefore wish to have them transmitted only at a local, regional or national level. The arbitration will have to recognise, at the very least, that in some cases the "equitable remuneration" payable for transfrontier distribution would be too high as a result of the extension of geographical boundaries and the considerable increase in the potential public, and that it would be appropriate not to require the programme to be transmitted internationally.

The question of quotas

A reading of the European Commission's Green Paper of 1984 which paved the way for the Directive might have led some to think that the main concern of the EC was not so much to facilitate the transmission of programmes across Europe as to ensure the free movement of commercial advertising on television, and to contribute in this way to the creation of an internal market for all goods and services. To allay this suspicion, the Commission, prompted by the European Parliament, included in its proposed Directive a chapter which did not feature in the Green Paper. It deals with "promoting the distribution and production of television programmes" and establishes programming quotas which require all broadcasting organisations of the Twelve to devote, within three years of the adoption of the Directive, 60% of their air-time to programmes produced in the Community. It also requires them to reserve one third of this time to first showings and to reserve 5% (rising after three years to 10%) of their programme budgets for programmes made by independent producers.

The principle of programme quotas provoked protests from most of the existing broadcasting organisations especially among EBU members who, in fact, generally observe comparable proportions in their transmissions. In their view, quotas take no account of the qualitative aspects of productions. They also maintain that any outside interference in the content of programmes would be an infringement of their autonomy. The survey by the European Institute for the Media[1] has shown that one state, France, already has a rigidly-structured programme and production quota system. Various other states already have laws, or are planning to have laws, detailing quota systems for indigenous programmes and/or production.In other countries, the broadcasting organisations have a mandate to promote their national culture, and this is laid down either in their charters or by statute. And where there are no quotas and where broadcasters do not have a specific mandate to promote national culture and national audiovisual production, they accept this mandate by imposing quotas on themselves for national programmes. The European Television Task Force takes the view that if legislative or regulatory provisions are not regarded as intrusions into the activities of broadcasters when they are made by national governments, the same must be true for requirements which would apply at the European level.

It also seems that the quota principle is compatible with the recommendations made by GATT: the dual cultural and economic nature of films and television programmes and the fact that the United States has a natural advantage by virtue of the size of its home market, give the authorities in Europe the right to demand specific exemptions without thereby creating obstacles which might endanger the free movement of ideas.

The majority of members of the Task Force believes that quotas for the production and transmission of programmes produced in Europe will have positive effects on the new audiovisual landscape of Europe. It seems that the television services operating at the present time, whether public or commercial, should not encounter any difficulties if such quotas are applied. On the contrary, quotas might help to protect them from the tough competition which some of the new operators of transnational or national television channels, whose main concern is commercial profit, would be tempted to undertake by the systematic use of low-priced non-European productions, which had already recouped their costs in other markets.

---

1   "Towards a European Common Market for Television: Contribution to the Debate", European Institute for the Media, Media Monograph No.8. Manchester, 1987 pp 53 to 58

One of the main criticisms levelled at the quota system related to the fact that the cultural scale of Europe exceeds the Member states of the Community. Any quotas for programmes produced in Europe which took account only of the Twelve would be misconceived from a cultural point of view. Again at the suggestion of the European Parliament, programmes originating from countries which are not members of the EC, but which are members of the Council of Europe or of EFTA, are now to be counted in the quotas on the basis of reciprocal agreements; in the same spirit, participation in co-productions is allowed in accordance with the same rules as programmes originating from the Twelve.

Further, the proposed Directive now states that what is classified as a "Community programme" depends not only on who produced and financed it, but also on whether the authors and workers engaged in it are resident in one or more member States (with the reciprocal arrangements mentioned above). This point is important: a production cannot be considered to be European merely on the basis of how it is financed. What matters is the work done by authors, artists and technicians from the various countries of Europe.

Competition and dominant market positions

The European Parliament had also proposed an amendment to the Directive intended to ensure that the provisions of the Treaty of Rome relating to competition were used to prevent the abuse of dominant positions. Such abuse could take the form of limiting pluralism and the freedom to broadcast information, as well as limiting information generally. A worrying problem in the ongoing development of the European audiovisual scene is the acquisition of interests in commercial television companies by groups whose financial power resides in other industrial sectors whose aim is often to dominate the media such as the press, publishing, records, radio, cinema and especially television.

In some countries, legislative provision has already been made for assessing and monitoring the involvement of such multimedia groupings. The European Television Task Force regrets that the amendment proposed by the Parliament to deal with this matter was rejected by the Commission on the grounds that the general provisions of the Treaty of Rome were sufficient and did not need to be repeated. Where culture and information overlap with economic considerations it will probably not suffice simply to refer to legal precedents relating to competition in the Community. Standards to be applied specifically to the audiovisual field will have to be worked out taking account of national laws dealing with the matter. The European Television Task Force hopes that these standards will be considered carefully and made known.

On the cultural level concentration can also have harmful consequences. A powerful transnational service could acquire exclusive rights to films and drama series, or to major sporting events, and thus handicap the national services (especially those of the smaller countries), lure away their audience and a large proportion of their resources. National broadcasters would then be compelled to rely mainly on second-rate material. The consequent reduction in their audiences and incomes would force them to give up the production of significant original work for lack of money.

Similarly, overall European production quotas do not by themselves guarantee that every country benefits equally from the obligation to use programmes made in Europe. Production capacity is very unequally developed: France, the Federal Republic of Germany, the United Kingdom, Italy and Spain possess, for both cinema and television, production resources which are incomparably better than those in the rest of the Twelve. The Single Act states that provisions to take account of these disparities must be available when the common European market is set up in 1992 and may be applied transitionally in any industry. Such provisions are certainly essential in the audiovisual field. European culture is made up of the national cultures of all member states, and does not consist of some elusive international culture.

The European Parliament, for its part, has pointed out quite fairly that the Directive, whatever its merits may be, is merely a first step towards the gradual and necessary development of a European media policy. It goes on to say that such a policy must not result in freedom of movement which allows would lead to the strongest organisations and the countries which have the most powerful and the highest quality resources for audiovisual production to become dominant. The Directive will therefore need to be accompanied by additional measures to moderate the disturbing effects of freedom of movement within the Common Market and to contribute to the maintenance and growth of the creative diversity which constitutes the wealth and the originality of European culture.[1]

---

1   Article 8C of the Single European Act states: "The Commission is aware of the enormous effort which some economies which are not all developed to the same degree will have to make during the period when the internal market is being established, and it can suggest appropriate measures. If these provisions take the form of dispensations, they must be of a temporary nature and disturb the working of the Common Market as little as possible"

The proposed broadcasting Convention of the Council of Europe

It might be thought that the Council of Europe is a more appropriate geographical grouping than the Europe of the Twelve for working out a cultural policy for the media. At the Vienna Conference in 1986 the participating communications ministers decided "to give the highest priority to bringing into being... binding legal instruments" to deal with some aspects of transfrontier television.

The Council of Europe usually acts through "recommendations". It cannot take decisions which are binding on the Member States, but the Committee of Ministers can draw up agreements or Conventions which − if they are adopted unanimously by the Committee − are recommended for ratification by the various Member States. Such instruments as Conventions are binding on a State when it has ratified them by passing a law or by some other formal act. The procedure is complex, but it does have the advantage that it can be implemented gradually. The Steering Committee on the Mass Media (CDMM) of the Council of Europe completed a draft Convention in April 1988 for submission to the Committee of Ministers.

The view has been expressed that through the proposed Directive and the proposal for a Convention, a regrettable rivalry has developed between the European Community and the Council of Europe. But, in fact, the Directive and the Convention cover largely the same issues. Like the Directive, the Convention recognises that the relevant law is that of the country from which a programme originates, and not that of the receiving country. Each State which is signatory to the Directive and to the Convention will have to ensure that all the programmes transmitted from its own territory conform to these instruments. This is what makes transfrontier transmission acceptable.

As far as general programme standards are concerned, the Convention is more precise than the Directive, but does not contradict it. The Convention, too, requires a right of reply to be provided. As for advertising, the rules of the Convention relating to specific products are more precise and more rigorous than in the proposed Directive. The daily limit for advertising is set at 15% of the total air-time, but a variant proposal which has not yet been approved states that this percentage should be raised to 20% for channels which offer viewers the possibility of buying goods directly (tele-shopping). The maximum advertising time per hour is fixed at 20% which is higher than in the Directive proposal. Sponsorship is regulated in the same spirit as in the

Directive. A number of variations are still being considered to limit the opportunities for inserting advertisements directly into programmes, but things seem to be moving in the direction of provisions which will have little compulsory force.

The Convention does not tackle the question of copyright and discards the idea of having quotas for European programmes. It restricts itself to general phrases, according to which each country that is party to the Convention should take appropriate measures to ensure that "a reasonable proportion of the time should be devoted to the transmission of television drama programmes, cinema films, artistic programmes, documentaries and educational programmes of European origin in order to encourage creative expression and to enrich the heritage and cultural diversity of Europe". It is still unclear whether the idea of a "reasonable proportion" will be defined in the explanatory report as meaning "the greater part of the time", or whether it will be left to the countries responsible for the transmission to define its meaning.

One article in the proposed Convention requires that each broadcasting organisation will be obliged to provide the authorities in its own country with name of its legal representative, an analysis of how its capital is made up, information about the nature and purpose of its programme services, and the method used to finance them. The title given to this article is "Transparency" and the explanatory commentary shows clearly that its aim is to make it possible to identify examples of the abuse of a dominant position. One of the reports presented at the Vienna Conference of the Council of Ministers in December 1986 had already pointed to the threat that multimedia monopolies may present to the free flow of information and thus to democracy. The resolution adopted in Vienna mentions that Ministers "have decided to forestall the monopolistic tendencies of the new television services". However, the obligation to be "transparent" is accompanied by only one rule which states that a broadcasting organisation cannot acquire exclusive rights of transmission or re-transmission which would deprive a substantial part of the public of following a major event on television. The European Television Task Force believes that additional provisions will have to be worked out to combat more actively cases of abuse of a dominant position.

Prospects for regulation

The Council of Europe and the Commission of the European Communities hope to bring the Convention and the Directive to a successful conclusion before the end of 1988. The Council of Europe now accepts that the Convention should be subordinate to the Treaty of Rome, and consequently to the Directive as far as the member

States of the EC are concerned. The Commission requires that the Member States of the Community give absolute priority to the Directive over the Convention.

But agreement on the Convention and the Directive has yet to be achieved. The April 1988 meeting of the Committee of Ministers of the Council of Europe left many questions undecided. It is not certain that a satisfactory agreement can be obtained on all the points to be discussed at the meeting of Ministers of Communication in November 1988, at which it is hoped to bring matters to a conclusion.

So far as the proposed Directive is concerned, the meeting in March 1988 of the Ministers responsible for the internal market showed that several countries still have reservations of a contradictory kind on a number of points. Some of these reservations relate to details of the quotas, while others indicate the unease felt by the smaller densely-cabled countries, such as the Netherlands and Belgium, which are in a particularly exposed position and which will thus experience immediately all the unsettling effects of the free circulation of programmes across frontiers on their home markets and their productive capacity.

The European Television Task Force is of the opinion that a number of provisions contained in the Directive or the Convention need to be amended, but that regulations formulated in the spirit of these two texts should be implemented without delay. It hopes that the greatest possible degree of compatibility will be established between the two texts. It hopes also that the provisions referring to European programme quotas will not be abandoned and will be accompanied by positive measures for supporting and encouraging creativity which are the essential complement to them. It hopes that both the instruments which are envisaged will be accompanied by a system for monitoring and enforcing the provisions which they contain.

Chapter 5
A dynamic European television industry

The substantial increase in the number of television services from which viewers can choose is likely to be no more than an illusion, if the schedules of the different channels are filled with the same imported or repeated programmes and the production of European programmes does not increase proportionately. The challenge which Europe must now face is to revitalise its programme production industry, and in particular that part of the industry which produces drama, or fiction. That this has not happened so far is indicated in Table 5.1, which shows that the increase in hours of broadcast on selected television services has paralleled by a reduction in the amount of in-house production of programmes.

The present and potential demand of television for new programme material is thrown into sharp relief by the fact that none of the twentyseven satellite services listed in Table 2.1 (Chapter 2) existed even seven years ago, nor did the new advertising supported services in Belgium, Denmark, the Federal Republic of Germany and France. What is more, existing television services are increasing their total hours of broadcasting, developing new overnight services and scheduling entertainment programming in hours previously unused. The consequent increased demand for programmes coincides with a rapid rise both in home production costs and in the cost of purchased programmes, as suppliers, particularly those from the United States, Australia and Brazil, find that their product is in greater demand and can command a higher price in a more competitive market. At the same time, there is evidence that the cinema industry throughout Europe, a traditional source of high quality fiction programming in most countries, has been suffering from a decline in cinema attendance, a reduction in the number of cinema seats available and a fall in the amount of cinema film produced in each year.

The link between the cinema and television industries is important. At the level of creative artists and skilled technicians there is increasing cross-fertilisation between cinema and television of people, ideas and techniques.

Table 5.1:
Development of broadcasting time and fiction production in some European broadcasting organisations

Broadcasting organisation		Development of broadcast transmission time 1975 - 1985	Development of own drama production 1975 - 1985
B	RTBF	+39%	-80%
D	ZDF	+28%	-4%
E	RTVE	+150%	-50%
GB	BBC	+14%	0
GB	ITV	+3%	0
I	RAI 1	+29%	-50%
I	RAI 2	+25%	-77%
		1980 - 1985	**1980 - 1985**
A	ORF	+18%	not available
F	TF1	+22%	-25%
F	A2	+20%	0
F	FR3	+26%	+18%

Source: A.LANGE "The Future of the European Audiovisual Industry",
Manchester, European Institute for the Media Media Monograph No. 10 (forthcoming)

At the same time, television is largely dependent on the products of the cinema industry for an important and popular part of its programming, as set out in Table 5.2.

The heightened competition for popular productions has two clear effects: firstly, the cost per hour for purchased programmes tends to rise as competition to secure them increases. Secondly, channel schedulers tend to favour programmes which cost less to bring to the television screen than do original productions but which can be counted on to attract a clearly defined audience: variety, game and chat-shows compered by star presenters, repeats of popular sports (such as the European Cup or World Championship Football, tennis tournaments, or Formula 1 racing), films made for the cinema, as well as series and serials.

It is evident throughout Europe that as the cost of programming rises, the amount of original material being produced or commissioned by the broadcasters reduces. If competition is allowed to take its natural course, and considering the wish of the commercial companies to maximise their profits and that of the public services to maintain their audience, there is reason to fear that the trends which are already discernible in some countries will become widespread in Europe, and will be strengthened by the growth of transfrontier transmission

The crisis in the European film industry

The number of films shown on the small screen is today increasing considerably in every country. Over the past two years the demand for, and use of, cinema film on television has increased sharply over the figures shown in Table 5.2.

In France, between 1985 and 1987, the annual average has almost doubled and even tripled if the pay-channel **Canal Plus** is included. In Belgium, where some twenty channels are available on cable, viewers can choose from between 60 and 90 films per week. To this must be added the growth in the video market, which relies mainly on films. The rate of growth of this market, too, varies from country to country, but is already significant: by the end of 1987, an average of 37% of European homes were equipped with a video recorder (see Table 2.4). The changes in living habits which encourage people to spend their leisure time at home or on the growing range of other available activities are reflected in falling box-office figures in cinemas throughout Europe. The decline in cinema attendance which became apparent in Europe in the 1950's but seemed to have stabilised at the end of the 1970's, began again in the 1980's, especially in Italy and Spain and, since 1985, in France, corresponding to the changes taking place in the television services. As a result there is little surprise in the fall by 30% in the number of feature films produced between 1975 and 1986.

The circumstances which made it possible for the production of cinema films to be profitable have drastically changed. From the beginnings of the cinema industry profitability depended mainly on the box-office; now, these receipts are proving to be quite insufficient and the important earnings are those from sales to television services, whether pay-television or open-access, and from video. If television is to continue to be able to draw on the cinema industry for a significant part of its programmes it is therefore important that the television channels invest more in the production or the co-production of new films, and that they increase the number of films and drama series which they produce. In a number of larger countries, such as Italy, the Federal Republic of Germany, France and the United Kingdom, the most powerful organisations are doing just this; but, overall, the number of original drama programmes shown by television is also declining on the public service channels, and is still small on the new commercial channels.

The financing of broadcast drama

Taking television programming as a whole, drama occupies a dominant place, both in the amount of air-time reserved for it and in its popularity with viewers. To a degree which varies from country to country, the dramatic content of the television schedule consists of films originally made for the cinema, or of made-for-television films and series. In general the made-for-television programmes are most likely to be ready-made purchased products rather than original productions made or commissioned by the service concerned. The reason is that the costs of producing drama — even when the programmes are not particularly ambitious — are among the highest in television. On average, it costs fifteen to thirty times more to produce or commission an original production than to buy the transmission rights to a film. What is more, during the last fifteen years, costs of drama production have grown more rapidly than the costs of other programmes. This is due particularly to the fact that audiences demand increasingly sophisticated and expensive production techniques, even for relatively modest programmes.

Of the films and series which are bought in, American products are by far the most numerous on all the television screens in Europe. There has for many years been a dominant American presence in European cinemas, reflected now in an increasing importance in the developing video market, but there is a growing reliance on American productions in television as well, as shown in Tables 5.3. On the various European channels, American drama represents between 35% and 55% of the total volume of drama transmitted. Indeed, films and series are often sold in packages: the acquisition of a recent successful and highly-priced film generally depends on the purchase of whole catalogues of products of variable quality, which substantially lower the average price. There is an abundance of material to choose from since, in addition to commercial films, the producers supplying the American networks can offer each year some 2 000 hours of "fresh product" in the form of series and TV films. For this reason, American programmes remain cheapest in terms of the cost/audience ratio,

Table 5.2: Use of feature films by European television services

Broadcasting organisation		Number. of feature films shown in 1985
A	ORF	769
B	RTBF	250
	BRT (1984)	*680
CH	SSR/SRG/TSI	845
D	ZDF	345
	ARD	379
	ARD 3rd channels	92
	SAT-1	*570
DK	DR	97
E	TVE-TV3	396
F	TF1	130
	A2	158
	FR3	212
	Canal Plus	*2300
	TV5	52
GB	BBC	810
	ITV	360
	Channel 4	380
	Sky Channel	*500
	Premiere	*1560
GR	ERT 1 & 2	*500
I	RAI (1984)	*830
	Reteitalia	2500
	other private services	*3000
IRL	RTE (1984)	*395
N	NRK	75
NL	NOS	200
	FilmNet	*1480
P	RTP	210
S	STV (1984)	*224
SF	YLE (1984)	*180
	MTV	*120

*Note: Figures marked * are estimated*

Source: A.LANGE, "The Future of the European Audiovisual Industry" Manchester, European Institute for the Media. Media Monograph No. 10 (forthcoming)

even if average prices have risen during the last few years as a result of the keener competition which is growing up between the European services.

What enables American drama programmes to penetrate the market is the fact that they have already recovered their costs on the home market; exports have only a marginal strategic importance. In 1984, exports, mainly to Europe, represented only 7% of overall receipts. It is also true to say that the size of the American domestic market, the consequent financial investment in programme production and the availability of the creative resources of the American film industry contribute in no small measure to the attraction of American productions. The same cannot be said for programmes made in Europe where, except in a few cases, the internal market in the country of origin is not large enough to make a film drama profitable and export earnings become an essential element in the production's finances.

Five European countries can be regarded as major exporters: the United Kingdom, France, Italy, Spain and the Federal Republic of Germany, with the first three maintaining a dominant position. The position of the United Kingdom is by far the most favourable: its receipts from exports in 1985 were 440.6 million ecu for cinema films and 187 ecu for television programmes; in France the corresponding figures were only 54 and 1.6 million ecu, in Italy 51 and 9.6 million ecu (see Table 5.4). The United Kingdom is also the only European country which derives more than 50% of its export receipts from the North American market (the United States and Canada); Italy obtains only 25%, France 18% and the Federal Republic of Germany only 9% (see Figure 5.5). In the case of the United Kingdom linguistic and cultural relationships play an important role: 23% of its export receipts come from Australia, New Zealand and Japan, and only 24% from Europe.

Only in exceptional cases do programmes from other European countries penetrate the United States market. This is because American viewers dislike sub-titled or even dubbed films. Generally speaking, the only European scripts which meet with success are those which are turned into new productions with an American director, American actors and all the necessary adjustments (cf. the recent *Three Men and a Baby*).

So far as programmes made in Europe are concerned, the countries of Europe form the most important market, but it is not an easy one to succeed in, since it is culturally and linguistically fragmented. In order to survive, the European film industry has long had to have recourse to various forms of government help. In a number of countries, this help takes the form of encouraging the public to invest in a high-risk industry, by offering tax relief based on a system of "tax shelters". These systems are organised in

Table 5.3:
Origin of fiction programmes
*(as a percentage of total amount of
fiction programmes broadcast in 1985)*

Broadcaster	Domestic production	EC Prductions	Domestic + EC	USA productions	Other productions
B RTBF	—	—	51	49	—
BRT[1]	21	46	67	33	—
D ZDF	17	33	50	36	14
SAT-1	20	31	51	48	—
RTL-Plus[2]	—	86	86	9	4
DK DR	7	43	50	46	4
E RTVE[3]	23	30	53	35	12
F TF1	22	34	56	37	9
Antenne 2	34	26	60	35	5
FR3	37	22	59	28	13
GB BBC[1]	38	7	45	55	—
ITV[1]	57	5	62	38	—
I RAI	11	28	39	57	2
NL NOS	7	30	37	56	7
P RTP	7	34	42	38	20

Notes:
1: 1982 figures
2: Estimate
3: Percentage of feature films transmitted

Source: A.LANGE "The Future of the European Audiovisual Industry" Manchester The European Institute for the Media, Media Monograph No. 10 (forthcoming).

a number of ways, which differ from country to country, but they allow private citizens and businesses to deduct from their taxable income — within certain limits — the sums invested in programmes made in that country.

To encourage capital investment, a law was passed in France in 1985 setting up the **SOFICA**, companies which manage investment funds intended to finance the production of films and audiovisual programmes. An *Institut du financement du cinéma et des industries culturelles* (IFCIC) is also able to provide the banking sector with guarantees to cover requests for credit made by new companies or by companies which are anxious to grow.

Often government help also takes the form of direct support at various stages of the industrial process. It may be provided for script-writing, or for the production, distribution, showing or export of programmes. Help may be automatic, and may be proportionate to receipts, and involve the obligation to invest in subsequent

Figure 5.4
1985 film and television export earnings of the three largest European audiovisual producing countries,
(in millions of ecu).

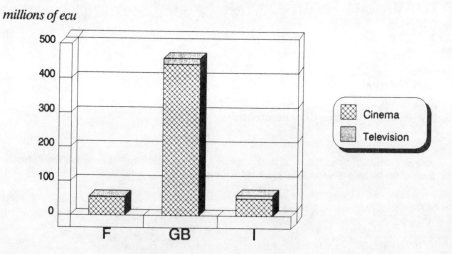

millions of ecu

Source: European Institute for the Media

Figure 5.5: Proportion of total 1985 audiovisual export earnings derived from the United States for the three largest European exporting countries

United Kingdom   Italy   France

Source: European Institute for the Media

productions; or it may be selective and take the form of an advance on receipts. Finance for these various kinds of help may come from State subsidies, but more often comes from a tax levied at variable rates and generally imposed on box-office receipts. This special tax is between 2.75 and 3.75% in the Federal Republic of Germany, 10% in Sweden, and 14% in France. This system makes it possible to set up a fund to support creative work by means of levies on the changing financial situation of the industry itself; in this way, in a number of European countries, American films which are widely shown in Europe help to finance the production of films made in the country concerned.

However the drop in cinema attendance has reduced not only the receipts from the showing of the films, but also the amount of money raised by the special taxes described above for the purpose of investing in new productions. In some countries, attempts have been made to make up for this loss by involving television companies in the production of films for the cinema.

Drama production in the European television industry

In 1974 in the Federal Republic of Germany the public television services **ARD** and **ZDF** signed an agreement with the FFA (Filmförderunganstalt) in order to avoid the imposition of legal restraints on their use of film material. The two broadcasting organisations have become part of the support mechanism for the cinema, by participating in co-productions, encouraging the development of new creative talent. It has been estimated that since 1974, both within the terms of the agreement and outside it, they have contributed in this way to the production of nearly 400 films; in 1985, of 64 films released, 34 were made with help from one of the public television services.

In Italy, where the commercial cinema has suffered particularly badly as a result of the considerable increase in the number of films shown by the multiplicity of private television services, **RAI** has for some years provided crucial help with the production of films whose qualities have received international recognition; in 1987, it put its investments at between 120 and 140 thousand million lire. The **ReteItalia** group, owned by FININVEST, which initially derived a substantial advertising income by transmitting many commercial films, imported drama series and cheap studio programmes, and which was regarded by its critics as digging the grave of the Italian cinema, has been expanding its production of drama since 1984; for 1987, it has invested 150 thousand million lire in the co-production of 65 films. these figures suggest that the ReteItalia group on its own accounts for between 30 and 40% of the overall investment in the Italian cinema. For 1988, FININVEST, which is the holding company of the Berlusconi group, has announced further expansion of its production activities, especially in France, where it has an important shareholding in La Cinq.

In the United Kingdom, the BBC and the independent television companies have always guaranteed that a certain amount of drama would be produced, but have mainly used their own production resources. In a spirit entirely in keeping with its deregulatory policy, the United Kingdom government in 1985 passed the Film Act, abolishing the Cinematographic Film Council, which was funded from a tax on ticket sales and expressed the view that the film industry should be subject to market forces. Since that time, an important area of support and seed money for new production has been **Channel 4**. a wholly-owned subsidiary of the Independent Broadcasting Authority (IBA), which has accepted a brief both to cater for minority and specialist audiences and to commission its programmes from independent producers and the ITV companies rather than making them itself. Channel 4 is not at present required to show a profit from the advertising which it transmits; its financial stability rests on the contributions to Channel 4 from the ITV companies. The level of these contributions is fixed by the IBA and effectively provides a fund for supporting the production of programmes.

In this sense, Channel 4 is a novelty in that it produces nothing itself; it co-produces programmes with foreign countries, and places orders with the IBA companies and especially with independent producers. By helping to encourage many small producers to undertake original creative work, Channel 4 is significantly assisting the film industry in the United Kingdom, mainly in the field of low-budget films. This model is now being followed not only by ITV companies but also by the BBC, which has changed its former policy of concentration on in-house production, and by other organisations elsewhere in Europe.

In France, since 1985, a levy on the resources of all the television services has provided an increasing proportion of the support fund for the film industry. This levy is made up of a percentage of the income which the commercial services receive from advertising or subscriptions, a percentage of the income which the public services receive from the licence fee and advertising, as well as a fee, paid as a lump sum by both the public service and commercial services, for every film shown. The money provided by the television services for the support fund increased almost tenfold between 1985 and 1987. Part of their contribution is devoted to supporting the programme industries in making TV films, drama series, cartoons and documentaries. The charters of the various services also impose quotas for programmes produced in the European Community, for original programmes made in French, and for "first showings" of dramas and documentaries. They require the various media to adhere to a prescribed sequence for the exhibition of cinema films: cinema release, followed by release on video, followed by showing on encrypted pay-television, and finally showing on open-access television).

The requirement to make original programmes laid down by the charters has already had positive effects, not only on the public service channels but also on the private sector. The pay-tv service **Canal Plus** has become increasingly involved in large-scale production, so offsetting the fact that its schedules are heavily dependent on existing cinema films, and the increased production commitment of **La Cinq** has already been noted above. However, programmes made by the commercial open-access services are not always profitable, leading to the suggestion that apart from TF1 the newer channels may not be in a position to fulfil the requirements of the charters under which they received their broadcasting concessions. When the commercial channels were set up under the law of September 1986, the French authorities laid particular stress on the opportunities which they offered to provide for the establishment of a focus for creativity in Europe, leading to substantial multinational participation by the Maxwell Communications Corporation in **TF1**, FININVEST in **La Cinq**, and the CLT (Compagnie luxembourgeoise de télédiffusion) in **M6**.

Even before it has begun to operate on direct broadcast satellite, **La SEPT**, which is described in detail in Chapter 6, has in its first three years commissioned and co-produced films costing more than 800 million francs.

One of the consequences of deregulating the traditional television system in Europe, and of the launching of commercial television stations in the various European countries, has indeed been the emergence of powerful groups whose interests originally were elsewhere than in the audiovisual industry: Havas was first involved in advertising, tourism and publishing; Bertelsmann in publishing; Berlusconi and Bouygues in the construction industry; Murdoch and Maxwell in newspapers (and the CLT, for its part, was long ago involved in the audiovisual industry). Most of these groups are trying to attract international capital, are creating links with one another, and are tending to form true multinational companies, in which audiovisual activities occupy one place among holdings of many kinds.

The aim of these groups was initially to gain control of broadcasting outlets, but they are tending to diversify their activities into the audiovisual industry, by means of production companies, or companies for distributing films or television programmes, for controlling cinema chains, cable-distribution or using satellites.

In the Grand-Duchy of Luxemburg, the CLT has had long-established subsidiary production companies for many years; but as Luxemburg is now witnessing the devolution of RTL's television interests to nationally-based organisations in France, the Federal Republic of Germany and Belgium (see Chapter 2) consideration is being given to the establishment, either by CLT or independent of it, of production companies which might attract foreign risk capital for the development of the audiovisual industry, and which could take advantage of the favourable taxation and banking laws in force in the Grand Duchy. Early plans in this area relate to participation in the production of American film series, an area where profitability seems least fraught with risks.

A similar strategy could also be adopted by other multinational groups, making films specifically intended for the American audience, shot in English, and with subjects, scripts and actors attractive to Americans. While such developments are of interest from the point of view of the industry, they are merely one aspect of the opportunities for expanding the audiovisual sphere: they do not serve the purpose of creating programmes which, from a cultural point of view, are specifically European.

As far as the future of original creative work is concerned, it would be unwise to place faith only in the multinationals of the audiovisual industry. Support must also be given to productions of various kinds which are being produced by film production companies established in different countries and by national television channels; they need to be organised into an effective European complex, by supporting or creating co-production initiatives, and by arranging for such programmes to be shown in a way which overcomes linguistic and cultural obstacles.

A promising response from European producers to this problem has been the establishment of formal co-production associations alongside the existing range of *ad hoc* co-production agreements traditionally made among independent producers and broadcasting organisations. There is a large, and growing, number of such co-production groupings, whose membership constantly changes; however, four representative examples are shown in Figure 5.6.

In the larger countries, the public television services, even if they have reduced the volume of original drama which they produce, continue to produce programmes specifically for television or, more and more frequently, are involved in co-productions for the cinema or television. Such agreements imply a search for solutions to the problems of multilingualism. But these initiatives are still very fragile. They need further support.

Initiatives taken by the Commission of the European Communities

The transnational showing of various programmes in the competitive context described above does not guarantee that the number of original programmes will increase. Measures are required which will provide active support for the expansion of the European audiovisual industry; they should be taken in parallel with the proposals of the Directive. The European Parliament has already made recommendations to this end. During 1985, the Commission worked out (using a Canadian model) a plan to set up a scheme which would provide financial help for drama coproductions involving at least three co-producers from different countries. In December of that year, however, the Council of Ministers felt unable to approve the proposal, because of the opposition of certain countries which refused to admit either the competence of the Community in the cultural sphere, or any systematic public involvement in the cultural industries. Since it was unable to put into practice a support scheme based on an aid fund, the European Commission put forward in 1986 "Measures to encourage the Development of the Audiovisual Industry"

(*MEDIA*). The *MEDIA* programme, whose initiatives will have to be financed mainly by interested partners, is designed to bring together resources and ideas for projects worked out by the professionals involved in production and distribution. So far as production is concerned, the major projects relate to areas which are particularly exposed to competition from outside Europe: the expansion of the new technologies (such as the production of images by computer), support for the animation industry, training in script-writing, and the use of funds for the promotion of creative work.

With regard to transmission, the *MEDIA* plan rightly addresses the problem of the linguistic divisions within Europe, which form a major obstacle to the movement of audiovisual material across frontiers[1]. A European fund for Multilingualism in the Audiovisual Industry is now being set up; it will initially be financed by the European Broadcasting Union (EBU) with a brief to provide financial support for multilingual productions, particularly in the less widely-spoken languages of the Community, and to contribute to the technical development of the procedures used for subtitling and dubbing. It has also been noted that most European films cross the frontiers of their country of origin, yet they need wider distribution throughout Europe if their profitability is to be assured. There are many films which the major distribution companies are not interested in distributing internationally because they are not convinced that they will be profitable. In this situation, producers and distributors from the twelve countries of the Community have worked out a model for a European Co-operative for the Distribution of Low-Budget Films. This model is based on a co-distribution mechanism receiving half of its income from advances on receipts and half from the distributors. It should be put to the test in the context of the *MEDIA* programme during 1988 by means of a pilot-scheme involving some fifty launchings of films in the Community.

The *MEDIA* Programme is also intended to contribute to the establishment of a promotion structure for independent producers in cinema, television and video, particularly in the major European audiovisual markets (the MIP and MIPCOM). Finally, it is intended to encourage a form of finance through the banking system which can work with the integrated production and distribution system which it is hoped to set up. The European Group for financing cinema and television (GEFCA), which brings together a number of European banking institutions, should act as a holding

---

1   For a detailed discussion of this subject see "Overcoming Language Barriers in European Television", Manchester, European Institute for the Media, (forthcoming).

Figure 5.6
European co-production organisations

ECA European Co-producers' Association, (founded in 1985)
Association of public service broadcasters:
Members: A2, RAI, ORF, ZDF, SSR, Channel 4, RTVE.

The European Consortium
Consortium of private sector broadcasters
Members: Silvio Berlusconi, Robert Maxwell, Jerome Seydoux

Vision
Association of independent producers
partners include Telecip and France Media International, with British, German and
Italian associates

EPC European Producers Corporation
Association of independent producers
partners are: FIT Film International Television Productions (F); Tele-München, (D);
Tangram (I); Lion (GB).

Source: "Broadcast", London, 22/4/'88

company for the various projects. At present the *MEDIA* plan, can take up only a
limited number of pilot schemes. but its effects will be multiplied significantly thanks
to the partners who are involved in its work.

Initiatives taken by the Council of Europe

In implementing Resolution 1 of the Vienna Conference (December 1986) of the
Ministers of Communications of the Member States, the Council of Europe is also
studying the measures to be taken to expand the production and co-production of
European audiovisual programmes, to promote initiatives in dubbing and sub-titling,
to further cooperation between the cinema and television, to encourage the
investment of private savings in the audiovisual industry by providing incentives, particularly in the field of taxation, to overcome the fiscal or administrative obstacles

standing in the way of co-productions of audiovisual programmes, and to promote the training of those who create programmes in the new audiovisual techniques.

The Council of Europe has also decided to involve itself in the establishment of a multilateral scheme for supporting film production and the programme industries, based on a French proposal following the collapse of the European Commission's project of 1985, described on page 89. Between nine and thirteen countries intend to participate in the scheme, which will allow assistance to be given for the co-production, distribution, transmission and promotion of works involving at least three different countries which are parties to the agreement, using contributions which will be determined according to a sliding scale on the basis of criteria such as the gross national product or the country's output of feature films. The states which are parties to the European Cultural Convention will be able to participate in this "European support fund for television and film production", which is to be called *Eurimages*, according to their resources and their needs. This fund, which will particularly favour the countries in which audiovisual production is less developed, will be under the control of the Council of Europe and will be managed by representatives from the participating states. These efforts made within the European Community and the Council of Europe to create a European audiovisual space are to be welcomed.

Direct and indirect help

In every European country, the film and television industry has had to ask for direct or indirect help with production. The mechanisms which govern these forms of aid work in a variety of ways and with greater or lesser effectiveness depending on the country concerned. Inside the Community, they could be criticised for the distorting effects they may have on competition when the single market comes into being; they could be criticised from outside for the same reasons. The European Television Task Force takes the view, however, that these forms of assistance are still essential today, that it would probably be appropriate to co-ordinate them and that they should be given a less nationalistic character and should be extended to cover European co-productions involving partners outside the Community on a reciprocal basis.

It is to be hoped that before 1992 the European Community will succeed in setting up the Fund to assist the audiovisual industry originally proposed by the European Parliament and the Commission. At present the European support fund described above is a good example of the way in which national schemes can be adapted to encourage co-production by a number of countries, and to improve the distribution and the international transmission of audiovisual programmes. The problem which still remains to be solved is that of providing the funding for international support schemes. Experience shows that state subsidies alone should not be relied on; political decisions are too delicate and too dependent on the hazards of circumstance. The European Television Task Force takes the view that mechanisms should be set up which guarantee this funding through levies imposed on the audiovisual sector itself. The national funds which work well rely, in fact, on a number of sources, including a percentage tax on cinema-ticket sales, or on private recording (videorecorders and recording accessories), a levy on the income of the television organisations (licence-fees, subsidies, advertising, subscriptions), a pro-rata contribution from the commercial films shown in cinemas and a levy on the income of the cable distributors. Sources of funding must also be set up which can constantly be renewed from the income of the sectors concerned, and the money used for advances on receipts or as non-recoverable funds both for co-productions and for dubbing and sub- titling, as well as for the distribution of programmes and for any other pre- or post-production operation. It should be understood that the television broadcasters contributing to the fund should have the right to use the productions in which they are interested, in proportion to their stakes, whether the programmes concerned are films or original work of other kinds.

Special attention should be given to audiovisual production in the smaller countries, whose output is limited. These should have privileged access to these support mechanisms. They should also be authorised to institute levies on the receipts of foreign television channels which transmit advertisements on their territory, on condition that these levies are devoted to the production and the promotion of national or European audiovisual programmes. In the same spirit, support for low-budget productions, which is proposed on an experimental basis in the *MEDIA* plan, should be increased.

Many countries encourage private citizens and businesses to invest in the high-risk audiovisual industry by offering tax relief through "tax shelter" systems. It is to be hoped that systems of this kind will be set up where they do not yet exist, and that the tax laws providing for these initiatives will be harmonised throughout Europe. The French *SOFICA* system (joint funds for investing in the audiovisual industry, enabling small investors to participate) is already arousing interest in various countries; it deserves to be tried elsewhere.

In view of the fact that the banking sector, while playing an active part in the new commercial television enterprises, is still reluctant to become involved in the production sector, it is an appropriate time to examine the forms of guarantee that can be provided (particularly via an *ad hoc* public organisation) to allay the fears of the banks and to encourage investment in the cultural industries. Finally, the harmonisation of the legal provisions designed to encourage co-productions between partners, and the consequences of harmonising the value added tax (VAT) regulations, should be examined.

There are substantial funds available in the mainstream commercial television industries of Europe, there is a wealth of creative talent in every country, and there is a substantial demand, not always clearly expressed, for European programming. What is needed now is that proper conditions should be created to encourage investment, stimulate talent and satisfy the demand of European television viewers.

Chapter 6
New European television services

The emerging range of options

The arguments listed in Chapter 5 for the development of a dynamic European film and television industry apply with even greater force to the development of genuinely European television services. In this chapter we consider the progress which has already been made along this road. We note that it is no longer appropriate to talk of one single European television service or even a single type of service. In practice, if one takes as the criterion of a European service the fact that it is broadcast with intent into two or more European countries, then there are already a dozen or more such services available, even though most of those are at present transmitted by low power satellites and, for this reason, viewable mainly in those areas where there are cable systems.

We are therefore dealing with an emerging transfrontier television system which runs parallel to the traditional national services. Viewers in Europe, at least in the metropolitan areas, already have available to them a dozen or more transfrontier television services transmitted mainly by satellite. Together with the terrestrial channels of national or neighbouring origin, the majority of European citizens will have access to 20 or more television programmes by the early 1990's.

It is evident from our knowledge of viewer attitudes that the viewers in general prefer programmes in their own language (see Table 2.3). Foreign language programmes will for some time continue to serve minority audiences, although in Scandinavia foreign language options have already achieved a substantial share of the audience, and appear elsewhere to have stimulated higher viewing levels overall. Such foreign language offers in the first place compete with each other and diminish only marginally the audiences for national programmes. If they are successful, it is mostly with special interest offers like news, sports or pop music. Research in francophone Belgium shows that programmes in French originating in France tend to be less attractive than Belgian programmes in French, and are widely used, essentially to watch feature films.

This suggests that if a European television service is to achieve a substantial audience it has to be available to each national audience in its own language, though European in content. All plans for European services should include a realistic approach to the solution of the language problem in as economic a way as can be developed. Five (English, French, German, Spanish and Italian), to eight (the first five together with Dutch, Portuguese and one or more of the Scandinavian) languages should be the objective for European services from the very beginning. Within each language region at least the relevant language version plus the original sound should be available.

The reality of European television already, as we have seen, exceeds the political arguments about the relationship between national and transfrontier services. Europeans are voting with their channel buttons, as yet in a small way but to a growing extent. Since at present most transfrontier services are provided by private entrepreneurs, it may be assumed that the economic grounds for their activities are sound. Three economic reasons account for these developments.

First there is the stimulus given to the European audiovisual industry resulting from increased demand for programmes from the new European channels. The existence of transfrontier services seeking audiences in a number of countries gives rise to more discussion and co-operation between producers in these countries. This, in turn, leads to a larger base for the audio-visual production industry, both as regards nationally based units and in terms of co-production arrangements.

Second, there is the catalytic effect of the growth in advertising expenditure (incurred as a result of the ability to advertise products on television across frontiers), on the development of trade in Europe in general. Little evidence is as yet available, but the arrival of new European television services supported by advertising will stimulate the development of pan-European products, and accelerate progress towards a common European market. The effect of the new transfrontier opportunities is already seen in the marketing plans of multi-national companies.

Third, there is little doubt that the provision of a television service which crosses European frontiers and which carries advertising across those frontiers acts as a direct stimulant to the advertising markets in all the countries in which such a service is viewed. The stimulation of overall advertising expenditure within one country by the addition of new advertising-supported television services is well documented. It is likely that these examples will be replicated to some degree by new trans-border advertising-supported television services. There is some evidence that this is already happening in the cases of **Sky Channel** and **Super Channel** even though these are monolingual and thus do not satisfy all the conditions of a European service.

Transfrontier audience research is in its infancy in Europe. One of the new research organisations, Pan European Television Audience Research (**PETAR**) estimates that viewers across Europe spend an average of 2.6 hours a week watching satellite channels. Which of these channels can be defined as European in their origin, content, presentation and reach is a different matter.

The first attempts to build a pan-European audience were initiated by **Sky Channel**, with transmissions by low power satellite from London starting in April 1982, and by the **Eurikon** experiment in the autumn of 1982. Since then, other attempts both in the public and private sectors have been trying to find their way in the intricate European scene, some of them by overcoming linguistic and cultural barriers, the rest being content to operate within the confines of regional or linguistic boundaries. These services cover a wide range of formulae, from general entertainment channels to national public services being distributed internationally. They include cooperative arrangements between public service broadcasters, commercially-offered thematic channels, and linguistically-based services (see table 2.1).

Existing public service provision

The public service sector experiences can be classified into several categories. The first is defined by the attempt to create a genuine European channel represented by Europa. The second consists of co-operative arrangements between public service broadcasters, both in the French-speaking (**TV5**) and the German-speaking (**3-Sat, Eins Plus**) areas. In addition, there is **Super Channel** which is described under the heading of commercially provided services due to its declared intent to operate as a commercial concern, although it was originally conceived as a co-operative project between the United Kingdom ITV companies and the BBC. The next group of channels being distributed in more than one European country consists of national services using satellite frequencies to reach beyond their national boundaries (**RAI-1** and **BBC1/2**). Lastly there are the proposals, as yet embryonic, for a European programme service of high quality.

Europa television

In 1982 the European Space Agency offered the European Broadcasting Union the use of a direct broadcast satellite planned for launch in 1986/1988 [1]. A number of EBU members investigated the possibility of establishing a pan-European multilingual television system. Their experiments were conducted under the code name **Eurikon**. The experimental phase culminated in broadcasts undertaken in 1982 by the **Independent Broadcasting Authority** (United Kingdom) **Oesterreichischer Rundfunk** (Austria), **RAI Radiotelevisione Italiana (Italy), Nederlandse Omroepprogramma Stichting (Netherlands), and ARD** (FRG). Other broadcasting organisations participated in the reception of the programmes, which were transmitted on the Orbital Test Satellite (OTS). The experiments included programming, organisation, strategic planning and relating the service to existing national networks. Four members finally agreed to cooperate in the operational phase: ARD, RAI, RTE and NOS, with RTP (Portugal) joining in June 1985. They formed a consortium with the aim of organising a multilingual European television service, to be transmitted via DBS satellite. Test transmissions of Europa began in October 1985 with NOS supplying a transponder on the European Communications Satellite.

Europa was managed by the Pan-European Satellite Broadcasting Consortium, open to accession by all active members of the EBU. Europa was financed by advertising revenue, members' contributions, the Dutch Government and the EC Commission. It offered advertisers flexible time schedules which allowed them to transmit commercials in different languages simultaneously to different national audiences. The advertisements themselves were transmitted in blocks between programmes, but not within them. The codes of advertising practice of the EBU, the Council of Europe and the International Chamber of Commerce were followed, thus avoiding any direct commercial influence on programme content.

During the first phase, until the end of 1987, Europa's programmes were distributed by cable systems receiving signals from the communication satellite Eutelsat 1, transponder 3, and over the air by the Portuguese TV network. Other European countries, which have no cable systems, were also able to transmit Europa on their terrestrial networks. Programmes were broadcast from Hilversum in Holland. It was intended that transmissions should be transferred to the European Space Agency's direct broadcasting satellite Olympus as soon as this was launched, giving good quality reception throughout most of Europe. Transmissions of Europa were made available

1   The launch of this DBS satellite, named OLYMPUS, has now been deferred to 1989

to cable licencees free of charge, down-link and copyright fees being paid by the service. The only expense to cable licensees was the reception and language-decoding equipment. With this licensees were able to offer Europa as an extra service to their subscribers. Europa reached over 6 million homes via cable and terrestrial transmissions during 1985/1986, the estimates for 1987/1988 being between 6 and 11 million. The expectations were that more than 30 million homes would be reached when direct broadcasting from the Olympus satellite became available.

The programming formula developed by Europa was intended to meet the following criteria: it had to be European, complementary, independent, universal and original. Programming reflected European culture and contributed to it. News coverage presented news important to the European audience as a whole, not from national points of view, but set in the wider European context. The complementary character of Europa meant that it functioned as a separate network alongside national services, transmitting high quality programmes from all the European broadcasting organisations. The problem of the different languages was solved by the transmission of several sound channels alongside a single vision signal. Subtitles were also provided by means of teletext. In this way, news and drama as well as sport and music were easily accessible and understood throughout Europe.

Europa offered the viewer an original concept: programmes from many countries, chosen and scheduled to provide a real alternative to national networks. The main evening programmes on each day of the week were devoted to a different theme. At other times of the day there was a range of quality programmes for children as well as extensive news, information and sports coverage. Initially five hours of programmes were transmitted each day, with eventual plans to increase to a full schedule running from early morning until late at night. Europa set high standards for itself both in programming and in technical expertise in order to provide an exciting and imaginative alternative to the national networks. It was developing a regular European television service able to attract a significant audience throughout Europe.

A number of factors contributed to the failure of Europa . The service opted for an evening-only schedule thus putting the service into competition with existing national programmes. The participating organisations were not in a position to provide productions for slots which they had undertaken to fill; nor were they in a position to guarantee the medium-term budget needed to develop the service's operations. The failure to see the service as a means of strengthening the role of international public broadcasting and to regard Europa as their own offspring prevented the national broadcasters from sharing the vision of international public broadcasting in addition to their national channels or satellite aspirations. The national public broadcasting organisations did not want to strengthen the role of the EBU from that of co-ordinating body to that of a network broadcaster with an executive role. National interests prevailed over the recognition of the need for a European experiment. In the absence of an adequate capital base to cover the pre-DBS period, the advertising sales operation needed a strong professionally experienced leadership, which could not be provided in the time available.

The difficulties suffered by Europa provide a great deal of experience of value to the next stage in the development of European services. The Europa service transmitted for an average of six hours per day in three and later four languages, subtitling being provided to Portugal from Hilversum on a daily basis. Programme acquisitions were kept within its financial budget. 60% were bought on the open market; 15%, mainly information and events, were produced in-house and 25% originated with the participating broadcasters. Europa developed strategies for obtaining European satellite rights and its negotiations with cable operators and advertisers on a pan-European basis was also valuable. The experience of working with an international programme staff appears to have been a success — national interests did not inhibit the search for a European identity. The preoccupation of the national parent services with the competition which Europa might present in the medium term appears to have led to their reluctance to enter financial obligations over a longer term. We conclude that European public services must be either independent of national public services or fully integrated with them.

Monolingual European services

Cultural aims have inspired two monolingual services which are transmitted by low-powered satellites throughout Europe[1]. They result from cooperation between national public service broadcasters. These are TV5 and 3-Sat. Each represents an attempt to promote and support throughout Europe a specific culture and language, in the one case the French, in the other the German. While both channels share this common characteristic, they differ in other respects.

TV5 is compiled from the contributions of five services belonging to francophone countries or regions: RTBF (Belgium); TF1, A2 and FR3 (France) and SSR (Switzerland), and also takes programmes from the Canadian Quebec consortium, CTQC.

1   In the case of TV5 the service also receives contributions from Télévision Québequoise and the
     service is transmitted in Canada

The channel's transmissions started in January 1984. It is financed by contributions from the partner countries. There is no advertising; there are no encoded transmissions; no subscription is required from viewers. The 1987 budget was 38.7 million French francs, France contributing 66%, half provided by the three national broadcasters and half by the French Foreign Office. Belgium, Switzerland and Canada contribute FFr 4.3 million each. Belgian and Swiss contributions are provided partly by the broadcasters, partly by the national telecommunications administrations while the Canadian contribution comes both from the CTQC and the Canadian government.

TV5 is intended to be a window for French-speaking culture revealing its diversity and plurality. The programming offered to European viewers was originally provided by each of the national public service broadcasters contributing one day of programming a week, TF1 and A2 providing Sunday programmes in addition, and hours not filled by the partners being filled with purchased programmes. This operating formula is being replaced by a more integrated one. TV5 is increasingly moving beyond its role as co-ordinating body and trying to develop a coherent policy which entails giving the partner organisations indications about the type of programmes they should provide for their allocated hours or days. These changes are accompanied by plans to increase TV5's own production, which up to now has been minimal. The medium-term objective is to increase the channel's penetration in European countries, with long-term plans for world-wide distribution. In 1987 TV5 was available to more than 6.2 million homes in Europe.

A different approach was adopted by 3-Sat, the German public service satellite channel which has been transmitting since December 1984. It is received in Central Europe with some significant audiences in Eastern Europe and the Middle East, particularly Hungary and Israel. Three public service broadcasters contribute to the service: the Federal German second network ZDF, Austria's ORF, and Swiss SRG. Headquarters are located in Mainz at ZDF, which meets administrative expenses, running costs and the transponder rental payable to the German postal administration.

In accordance with ZDF's charter the aim of 3-Sat is to promote and support German culture. Its target coverage area does not at present extend beyond Germany, Austria and German-speaking Switzerland. Unlike TV5, programme hours and days are not distributed between the three partners. 3-Sat operates a common programme schedule into which different contributions are fitted. Programmes are provided by each of the broadcasters; ORF contributes 35% of the total output, SRG 10% and the rest is provided by ZDF. The service broadcasts around 20 minutes a day of live programming and has plans to increase this figure. Repeats of terrestrially transmitted programmes amount to 45%. At present, 3-Sat is available to almost 3 million homes in the Federal Republic of Germany (2 300 000), Switzerland (374 000) and Austria (290 000). The service carries no advertising.

Since 1986 the German ARD and the Swiss Broadcasting Corporation have also been transmitting a German-language cultural service **Eins Plus** from Intelsat V, a low powered satellite. The service transmits programmes first shown on ARD's first and third programmes.

International distribution of national services

Besides the co-operative arrangements described above, public service broadcasters make their presence felt in the European arena by beaming national services via satellite into other countries and operating in a way similar to the American so-called "superstations". These are local or national services whose programmes are transmitted by satellite beyond their terrestrial areas of reception. There are examples both at the national and the international level. The German regional channels **WDR3** and **BR3** are transmitted by satellite to other regions in the Federal Republic. At the international level, **RAI Uno** of Italy and **BBC1/2** of the United Kingdom are examples of national channels being received in other countries. RAI has a large audience among expatriate Italians in Belgium, Switzerland and Luxemburg. In these and other countries, programming is distributed by local cable systems. At the same time, the channel is available by direct reception (TVRO and SMATV) all over Europe. BBC1/2 (a mix of these two British channels) has made arrangements for distribution by cable in six European countries.

A European service of high quality: La SEPT

A European culture-oriented channel will provide European viewers with a service complementary to those offered by the national broadcasting organisations. Cultural events, documentaries, films, music, dance, plastic arts, opera, science, technology, are the various ways in which national and European culture is expressed. With this aim in mind, a first attempt is being organised by **La SEPT**. This service defines itself as a cultural channel of French initiative, intending to build its pan-European audience with a programme of high-quality and of European interest.

M. Pierre Desgraupes, the former Director General of Antenne 2 was asked by the French Government in 1984 to design such a service. His report recommended that the service should transmit programmes of European origin and live broadcasts of events in several languages as well as encouraging co-operation and co-production between European broadcasters. The channel would concentrate on programmes of interest to a European audience. It would carry films (23%), entertainment (20%), information (12%), music (8%), children's programming (10%) documentaries (8%) drama (6%) and sports (6%), of interest for a common pan-European audience. Although M. Desgraupes' project was not implemented because of the high costs involved, most of its principles have been adopted by **La SEPT** (*Société d'Edition de Programmes de Télévision*), created in 1985. La SEPT is not a production company. It commissions programmes or buys them. The financial structure and organisation are at present French but are intended to expand into a European organisation. At present financial resources are provided by the French Government (25%), FR3 (45%) INA (15%) and Radio France (15%). Participation by ARD and ZDF in the Federal Republic of Germany is being sought.

Transmissions are still in their experimental phase. Until the launch of the French direct broadcasting satellite TDF1, La SEPT is using FR3 transmitters for 160 hours of programmes between SEPTember 1987 and June 1988. On TDF1 it will transmit eight hours of programmes rotated three times a day so as to provide a 24-hour service. The European character of La SEPT is manifested by the priority given to multilingual operations and to co-productions. Co-production agreements have been signed with ARD and ZDF (Federal Republic of Germany), SSR (Switzerland), RTBF (Belgium), Danmarks Radio, (Denmark), ORF (Austria), NDR (Federal Republic of Germany), RAI (Italy), RTVE (Spain) and RTE (Ireland). Programmes will be transmitted in the original language version with subtitling in several languages. La SEPT's cultural aims are reflected in the programme schedules which include documentaries, light entertainment and drama, as well as a substantial proportion of educational programming, including foreign language teaching. Each Sunday evening is devoted to a special event broadcast live from the country of origin. In 1987 more than 1 000 hours of French and European programmes were commissioned or bought.

Commercially funded services

In the absence of direct high or medium powered satellites it is as yet unclear how many channels will be able to compete and survive in Europe. So far the field is being tested in several ways by low power satellite transmissions which are receivable mainly through cable systems. Some services provide the audience with general entertainment services while the others try to make their way as thematic services aimed at specific audiences. All services are financed either by advertising and sponsorship (**Super Channel, Sky Channel, Sat-1, RTL Plus, MTV Europe**) or by subscription (**FilmNet**), or a mixture of both (**CNN, Children's Channel, Lifestyle**, etc). The details of share ownership, hours of transmission and number of homes connected for all these services are contained in Table 2.1.

General entertainment channels

The most successful and widely-distributed general entertainment services up to now are **Sky Channel** and **Super Channel** which are available to over ten million households in more than 15 countries across Europe. Neither of them has reached its break even point yet, principally due to the problem of attaining maximum distribution (see below). Both are English-language based channels, oriented towards the family audience. Sky Channel has no particular national affiliation; Super Channel transmits mainly British programmes contributed by the BBC and Independent Television. Both channels are distributed on cable networks and SMATV.

Satellite Television plc which transmits the **Sky Channel** service across Europe, was established in London in October 1981. Investors, all from the United Kingdom, included merchant banks Barclays and Guiness Mahon, the leisure interest firm Ladbrokes and the Scottish publishers D.C. Thomson. Transmissions lasting two hours per day began in 1982 on the OTS-2 satellite. They were receivable by cable networks in Norway, Finland, Malta and Switzerland. In 1983, News International plc purchased 65% of the channel and a contract was signed with British Telecom to lease a transponder on the new European communication satellite (ECS-1). In 1984, the new brand name of Sky Channel was adopted and the service began to be distributed in the United Kingdom, Germany, Austria, the Netherlands and Sweden as well as increasing transmission hours to 8 per day. IN 1985, it entered the cable market in Luxembourg, France and the French-speaking region of Belgium

The first pan-European audience survey conducted by Sky/AGB in February 1986 showed the increasing penetration of the channel. A second survey, by Pan-European Television Audience Research (PETAR), showed that by March/April 1987, Sky Channel was reaching 92% of the cable homes surveyed across 12 countries. By January 1988 it was available to 11 million homes (30 million potential viewers) in 19 countries (Austria, Belgium, Denmark, Federal Republic of Germany, Finland,

France, Greece, Hungary, Iceland, Luxemburg, Netherlands, Norway, Portugal, Spain, Sweden, Switzerland, United Kingdom and Yugoslavia).

The service offers entertainment programming consisting mainly of serials and made-for-television films (51%), light entertainment (33%), feature films (10%), and sport (6%). Only one programme a week, the *Roving Report*, is devoted to news and current affairs. Besides this, arrangements have been made to include programming from some of the countries receiving the signal. New productions amount to around 41% of the total programming output (early 1986), and in January 1987 about 38.2% of the programming is originated by Sky Channel at its own production studios. Only half its programmes (54% by mid-87) are of EC origin. Further penetration in European countries depends on the removal of technical, regulatory and linguistic barriers. Sky Channel is trying to overcome the latter by including subtitling, in particular for the Dutch audience (3 226 404 homes connected in mid 1987). The regulatory issue is approached with care, trying to avoid any reference to carriage-fees. The next major enlargement of coverage depends on satisfactory direct broadcast facilities becoming available.

The idea of the ITV satellite service **Super Channel** was first discussed in 1983 but no action was taken until 1986. Super Channel started transmissions on ECS-1 on 30th January 1987 as an advertising-supported 24-hours-a-day channel. A PETAR survey only six weeks later showed that the channel's penetration was 74%. Initially Super Channel had been intended as a channel offering the "Best of British" programmes supplied by the BBC, the United Kingdom Independent Television companies and Channel 4. However, the experience of Music Box and Sky Channel showed that such a mono-cultural approach was unlikely to win large audiences in European countries outside the United Kingdom. For this reason the programme schedule, while retaining mainly British programmes, was designed to meet the expectations of a non-British European audience with a knowledge of the English language. It included a daily half hour news bulletin, a European weather report, *"What the Papers Say"* from Granada and the monthly magazine programme *"Piazza"* covering various aspects of the European Community. Owing to a shortfall of advertising revenue during 1987 the 1988 budget was reduced from £26 million to £19 million. Transmission time was reduced to 21 hours per day, reducing the number of hours of Music Box programmes and the length of news bulletins. Programme expenditure was concentrated on the hours between 1600 and midnight; and more effective acquisition and scheduling of programmes for the multi-national audience was achieved. More emphasis was placed on action and less on programmes involving speech; additional American and Australian programmes were acquired. The service's output, however, remains more than 80% European. With the new Dutch and German programmes shown with English subtitles the service now claims to be "for Europeans made by Europeans".

SAT 1 is a less widely-distributed general entertainment service which started operating for 21 hours per day on the Ludwigshafen pilot cable network, with the backing of some of Europe's most powerful and successful publishers. Penetration on German and Austrian cable networks increased between 1985 and 1986. In a second stage, the channel moved into a combination of cable and terrestrial distribution in Germany, after the release by the Deutsche Bundespost in July 1987 of extra primary frequencies in 100 towns and secondary ones in 65 towns. The latest projections by SAT 1 suggest that the channel will be available to 20 million viewers by the end of 1988.

Thematic services

Thematic services were first seen in Europe in 1984 with the development of cable networks in the United Kingdom and Germany and with a terrestrial popular music service in Italy. The services are modelled on cable channels in the USA and aim to attract specific segments of the audience (children, young people, women), or special interest groups (sports, films, the arts). Most of these services aim to attract segments of the audience whose numbers at the national level are too small to be viable but which can become so as part of the larger audience reached by transfrontier signals. None of these channels is as yet profitable, principally due to distribution difficulties. The thematic channels include **Children's Channel, Screensport, Lifestyle, Arts Channel, FilmNet, CNN, Worldnet** and **MTV Europe**, all of which have a small multinational audience; and **Premiere, Videomusic** and **Canal J** whose audiences are currently restricted to one country, but which hope to enlarge their coverage in the future. However, one such service, **Teleclub**, ceased operation early in 1988.

News and Information

The quest for a European news service made in Europe continues. A proposal is under discussion in the EBU but has not, at the time of writing, reached the stage of a formal proposition. The most widely distributed thematic service providing only news and information is **Cable News Network (CNN)**, the leading news channel in the US with 38.2 million home connections there in April 1987. After five years of success in the United States CNN entered the European arena in September 1985. It broadcasts 24 hours a day live worldwide news and features on business and financial matters, health, entertainment and fashion, compiled from its US news service, with the addition of some material specifically aimed at a European audience. There are plans to launch a service oriented entirely to European viewers, as well as a financial data service.

Though intended to expand further into the cable market, CNN started its penetration of Europe via to the SMATV market (particularly hotels) and by selling its news material to national broadcasters. The latest of these national broadcasters to subscribe to the service are RTVE (Spain) and the Polish Television network TVP, the first broadcasting organisation in a socialist country to subscribe to CNN. The channel's main source of revenue in Europe is sales of material to national broadcasters. At present the service is received on cable and SMATV systems in Ireland, Sweden and the United Kingdom, with a lower penetration in France and Denmark. It is also available in about 23 000 hotel rooms.

A second US presence in Europe in the field of television news and information is **WorldNet**, the information service run by the United States Information Agency. It is provided free to cable operators. There is no advertising, the service being fully funded by the USIA budget. In 1987 this amounted to $19 million for the world operation and $4 million for the European operation. WorldNet offers US Government news reporting, sports, science and cultural programming, with some English language teaching. It transmits from 0700 to 0900 and from 1200 to 1600 hours Central European Time (CET). These are convenient times for cable operators and make the service suitable for channel-sharing. Worldnet began operations in April 1985 and first transmissions in Europe began in April 1987. It is intended to increase transmissions to 12 hours per day by the end of 1988. At present the service is linked to more than 2 million households in several European countries. As no audience surveys have been conducted it is not known to what extent the service is watched by European viewers.

Popular music

Besides the large quantity of pop video material transmitted on Sky Channel and Super Channel, as well as other channels distributed at the national level (**Tele-5** on German cable networks and the 24-hour-a-day **Video Music** in Italy) attempts have been made to launch pan-European music channels. These are **Music Box** and **MTV Europe**. **Music Box** started transmissions in June 1984 as an advertising-supported service offering 24 hours a day of pop music, videos and concerts. After reaching a high level of penetration which was not reflected in a relatively low level of advertising, the Music Box service was replaced by Super Channel in 1987 (see above). The new company, Music Box Limited, has become a successful music programme provider after only one year. It provides programmes to broadcasters all over the world including one hour per day to NHK's DBS service in Japan and one hour per week to a USA Cable Network. Over 90% of the content of Music Box last year consisted of new production, mainly of European origin (77% EC content).

The second attempt is **MTV Europe**, modelled on the format developed by MTV, a successful channel received by more than 33 million homes via more than 4 000 local cable systems in the US. MTV Europe is intended to be tailored to European interests; only a small proportion of the 24 hours of programmes per day will be the same as the programming distributed in the US. Transmissions of MTV Europe started in August 1987. Three months later, the service claimed nearly 3 million households and seemed to find its main audience in the under-34 age group. The service is owned by a consortium of Mirror Newspapers (United Kingdom) (51%), British Telecom (24%) and Viacom International (25%), the owners of MTV in the USA. Viacom provides the service with its large stock of concerts, video clips and animation. In spite of the rapid growth in distribution, it is as yet uncertain how far the service's American style will suit the musical tastes of European viewers and attract advertising, its sole source of revenue.

Children's Programmes

The **Children's Channel** started in June 1984 as a service funded by Thorn EMI Cable Television to provide the United Kingdom cable networks with a children's entertainment channel. Ownership was transferred in 1986 to a new company, Starstream Ltd, now owned by British Telecom (22%), Central ITV (22%), D C Thomson (22%), Thames Television (22%) and Thorn EMI (12%). The service started expanding to Finland (Helsinki Cable TV) Sweden (Televerket cable networks), Denmark and the Netherlands, with plans to enter Ireland, Belgium and Norway in 1987-88. The service receives its revenue both from subscriptions and advertising. Blank-out ads [1] are sold in each country of transmission. Problems arising from differential restrictions on advertising have been solved by replacing breaks with teletext pages using teletext decoders installed at the cable headend.

---

1   Advertising breaks from which the original advertising has been removed.

The French **Canal J**, which started operations in January 1986 and is distributed at present on Telecom 1B had 28 000 connections in the French market by the end of 1987, with plans to expand into the French-speaking area of Belgium. Since the language problem can, in the case of child audiences, be determinant, Canal J avoids subtitling, which seems to be discriminatory when used with young audiences. On the other hand, the high costs of dubbing have caused this channel to avoid foreign productions and to concentrate its programming on domestic and French-speaking productions.

Other services providing for child audiences are being planned, and one such service, **Kindernet**, was launched in March 1988 in Belgium and the Netherlands, financed by a charge levied on the cable operators themselves. This service is intended to share a transponder with Lifestyle and Screensport.

Sports Services

Screensport is a sports channel started in March 1984 to serve the United Kingdom cable networks. It is funded from subscriptions, advertising and sponsorship. The main shareholders include WH Smith (87% at January 1987), the American sports and information network ESPN, ABC and Ladbroke Group. The sport-only formula has proved successful in the US. ESPN is in fact the largest satellite-to-cable network, with over 40 million subscribers on over 15 000 networks. Screensport had a weaker programme offer at the beginning, with minority and esoteric sports occupying large parts of its schedule. Since 1986, however, the service has moved into the international arena. It has entered the Nordic countries and is trying to penetrate the large cable networks in the Netherlands as well. The service has been trying to improve its image by incorporating coverage of soccer, ice hockey and water sports, although it is still far from being able to buy the cable and satellite rights for world events. The proportion of non-EC productions has decreased, from 54% in 1986 to 27% in 1987.

A French sports channel is currently at the planning stage to serve the French, Belgian and Swiss cable networks. This new service, called **TV Sport**, will be the French replica of the English language Screensport. WH Smith will also be the main shareholder in this service.

At the time of writing, negotiations are virtually complete for the establishment of a pan-European sports service to be operated by a consortium of the European

Broadcasting Union and News International. The exact details of the service have not yet been made public but it is known that participating member organisations of the EBU will offer sports coverage for which they have rights but which cannot be fitted into their current schedules, as well as shared coverage of a number of national and international events.

Film services

Pay-TV services in Europe have been modelled on the North American examples of Home Box Office and The Movie Channel. However, differences between the European and the US markets have emerged. Both European linguistic plurality and regulatory fragmentation in such fundamental areas as copyright have made the development of film services more difficult. At present, European experience with such channels is limited to services which are linguistically-based and regionally-distributed, the most important of which are **Premiere**, showing new films in English to the British audience, and **FilmNet**, intended principally for viewers in the Benelux countries and Scandinavia. **Premiere**, with backing from Maxwell Communications Corporation, 20th Century Fox and Columbia Pictures, and the two United States market leaders in cable film service HBO and Showtime: The Movie Channel, uses an encrypted signal to reach its 40 000-odd subscribers in the United Kingdom.

FilmNet seems to have had most success in widening its distribution. At present, it is the main multi-national, multi-linguistic premium channel distributed in two main areas: Benelux and Scandinavia, with more than 200 000 subscribers in six countries. It has plans to expand to the French market and expects to reach break-even point by the end of 1988 with 300 000 - 350 000 subscribers. FilmNet began transmissions in the Netherlands and Sweden in the Spring of 1985, expanding into other countries shortly after. The service is a joint venture between the Swedish conglomerate Esselte, VNU and UIP (the two latter participating only in FilmNet Holland). The 24-hour schedule is divided into three programming sets which can be selected by the viewer separately or in combination. FilmNet offers a new title every day, with a film starting every two hours and frequent repetitions. About 2 000 films are shown each year. Since the channel is aimed at a multi-lingual audience in six countries, subtitling has become an important feature. Subtitling is currently available in Dutch, Danish, Swedish, Finnish and Norwegian using the Esselte Multi-Subtitling System (EMSS), which allows the cable operator to chose which subtitle appears on viewers' screens. Though the main market for FilmNet is the cable market, it has also devoted attention to the TVRO market, adapting itself to direct-to-home reception by renting decoders to TVRO's owners. As yet only about 2 000 subscribers receive the service via TVRO throughout Europe. Besides the cable and TVRO market, the channel is transmitted terrestrially on Kanal 2 in Denmark.

Canal Plus, the French-language film, sports and entertainment service, is beginning to expand its coverage to French-speaking Belgium and Switzerland. Thus it will in due course become a transfrontier service and qualify for inclusion in this survey.

The remaining service falling into this group is **Teleclub**, which was directed to the German-speaking part of Switzerland, but ceased operations early in 1988.

The Arts and Culture

Apart from the planned developments of **La SEPT** already discussed above, the only attempt so far to initiate a transfrontier service specialising in the arts and culture is The **Arts Channel**, at present available to over 600 000 cable homes in the United Kingdom, the Netherlands and Scandinavia. The owners include WH Smith and Television South (United Kingdom), among others. Satellite transmissions began in September 1985 with two and a half hours a day being transmitted from 0600 to 0830 in the morning for recording and replay by cable operators and VCR cable homes. More recently, The Arts Channel has been transmitted at the end of the nightly Sky Channel service, with a consequent increase in the number of European homes to which it is available. The Arts Channel offers a mixed programme of opera (15%), dance (7.5%), drama (10%), jazz (6%), classical music (25%), documentaries and visual arts (over 35%). Most of the programmes are of European origin (84% in 1986, 77% in 1987). About 85% of the material is bought in, some programmes being provided free. Programmes are rerun about five times a year.

The main problem the service faces is financial. It has a good reputation as a non-advertising, cultural service. This has enabled it to enter cable markets in the Netherlands and Scandinavia. However, it seems to be far from breaking even. Viewing figures are very difficult to obtain; it may well be that the audience is even smaller than assumed.

Women's Programmes

The feminine audience is also of interest to programme providers. They have tested the field in Europe with **Lifestyle**, similar to the US cable network Lifetime, which at present reaches 30 million TV homes on 4 700 cable networks across that country.

Lifestyle started transmissions in October 1985 and aims to attract the feminine audience. The schedules include chat shows, health, soap operas and cookery programmes. The service is owned by WH Smith (47%) D.C. Thomson, Yorkshire Television and Television South, the two latter companies being the main providers of programmes for the service.

Since the end of 1986 the **Lifestyle** service has expanded into other countries, particularly Sweden and the Netherlands. At the same time, it increased its imports from the USA so as to attract a larger audience among those enjoying US soap operas and romantic drama. Consequently the European content of Lifestyle declined from 55% in 1986 to 37% in 1987, while the schedule has been increased by two hours a day. This has meant that Lifestyle could share a channel with **Screensport**, the end of transmission hours on one coinciding with the starting time of the other. In order to test the possibilities for a 24-hour home shopping channel, a formula which is proving very successful in the US, Lifestyle has started a half-hour, three times a week, home shopping trial. It is not yet known whether there exists a European market for this type of service, although there are examples of such services being transmitted terrestrially in Italy, France and Germany.

Religious programmes

Religious and family-oriented networks, generally with sectarian Christian objectives, are a characteristic phenomenon of US television. Some of them, like the Christian Broadcasting Network with 34.5 million connections in 1987 are among the most widely distributed services on US cable networks. This phenomenon has not yet reached Europe on a large scale. The **New World Channel**, owned by Evangelical Broadcasting Network (EBN), provides one hour (rebroadcast three times) of religious, family-oriented, programmes a day. These are mostly American-produced and are distributed in a variety of local languages. No viewing figures or penetration data are known, but the service appears to have connections in Belgium, Finland, France, the Netherlands, Norway, Sweden, Switzerland and the United Kingdom. The main stream churches of Europe are anxious that sectarian evangelism by television may make inroads on the relatively high-quality tradition of religious television developed in Europe.

Television organisations operating outside their country of origin

The survey of European commercially-provided services would not be complete without a reference to multinational enterprises operating national services in different countries, generally with local partners. The internationalisation of investment in the television industry is treated in Chapter 2 (p.24-26); here we are concerned with the impact of this development on the provision of television services outside the home country of the organisation. The Compagnie luxembourgoise de télédiffusion (CLT) operates such services in France (**M6**), Belgium (**TVi**) and the Federal Republic of Germany (**RTL Plus**), as well as in Luxemburg and the Lorraine region of France (**RTL**). The Italian FININVEST company, besides owning three national networks in Italy, is a major partner in **La Cinq** (France), **Tele-5** (Federal Republic of Germany) as well as in the important Spanish film production centre Roma Studios.It also holds the concession for the sale of television advertising from Western countries in the Soviet Union. The **Maxwell Communications Corporation** (United Kingdom) has cable interests in Britain, is a minority shareholder in **TF1** (France) as well as in one of the potential applicants for the commercial television franchise in Portugal. The Federal German Bertelsmann AG has a major share in **RTL Plus** as well as media and publishing interests in France and the United States of America. The progressive merging of private media interests in Europe into a small number of multinational enterprises is beginning to give cause for concern on account of its potential consequences for the maintenance of media diversity and freedom of expression.

A variation on these activities are the enterprises which circumvent the laws governing television in one country by transmitting programmes from another country. The Scandinavian **Scansat** service is an example of a multi-lingual, regionally oriented, project financed by **Kinnevik**, the largest shareholder after the Luxemburg Government in Société européenne des satellites, the operators of the ASTRA satellite due to be launched at the end of 1988. Scansat at present rents a transponder on Intelsat V and began transmissions of **Scansat 3** addressed to Danish and Swedish cable networks in January 1988. When the SES ASTRA medium-powered satellite is launched, Scansat will use its transponders to build up a Swedish, a Norwegian and a Danish language service encrypted from the uplink and distributed simultaneously into the three countries. It is a Scandinavian alternative to the national public service programmes which as yet maintain their monopoly in Norway and Sweden. Scansat intends to provide 40-45% of Scandinavian-produced programmes within five years and hopes thus to compete with the increasing range of programmes coming from abroad.

A further recent example of this type of activity is the transmission, also from the United Kingdom, of **Canal 10** to Spain. This commercial service transmits in Spanish only and aims to pre-empt the proposed legislation governing the deregulation of television in Spain.

European Television Services in the Public Interest

This brief survey of the emerging options in the range of European television services suggests that little incentive is needed in the private sector. The potential return on investment in commercial services appears to be adequate to bring new entrepreneurs into the field. It is the more unfortunate, therefore, that the one specific attempt made so far to create a European public television service had to be discontinued for lack of resources. The European Television Task Force is convinced that this is not the end of public service television on a European scale. We recommend here that multilingual European television services working in the public interest should be established just as, in Chapter 3, we recommend that the national public service broadcasting organisations should be assured of the resources necessary to provide and develop the full range of their service.

The Task Force takes the considered view that within a spectrum of European services there should be scope for more than a single service operating in the public interest. We have already identified the need for a general service of high quality as well as for a European news and current affairs service.

The nature of these services is closely linked to the ownership and control of the service. Possible models of ownership are

● a public corporation;

● a joint venture enterprise employing private and public capital;

● a privately capitalised enterprise.

Whichever is chosen for any service, both capital and revenue funding will have to be provided from one or more of the following sources to produce an annual income of the order of 120 million ecu.:

- A European licence fee could be levied on both cable connections and TVRO dishes. Because of the number involved, the amount of such a charge would not need to exceed the equivalent of 10 ecu per house/year (120 million ecu per year). The fee might conveniently be collected through the cable operators themselves or, in the case of TVRO dishes, through the licensing authorities in each country.

- A share of the national licence fees would be justified if the European services were made available to national television services. 5% of these fees from 120 million households would produce income of the order of 450 million ecu per annum.

- Direct subvention from the European institutions. There might be objection to the provision of the 120 million ecu per year that would be needed properly to operate a service. The engagement of start-up funding over a ten year period from the Institutions might be linked either to shares in the operating company or to debentures repayable after the tenth year.

- Contributions from national broadcasters could be made in two ways: by providing the service with the necessary financial support or by providing goods and services. The Europa Television experience suggests that unless each contributor commits his organisation to specified duties and obligations in advance, this mode is unlikely to provide sufficient stability to operate a viable service.

- Advertising and sponsorship will be a useful source of income where a clearly identifiable audience segment can be attracted and sufficient distribution obtained.

- The feasibility of subscription as a means of funding depends on the ability to provide value to the subscriber and on the number of subscribers.

- It would be possible to raise funds for European channels by means of a European lottery. Moral objections to this are likely to be raised in some quarters.

- A further source of funding would be the publication of a magazine or series of magazines listing programme details of the services alongside listings of other national or transnational services.

It is emphasised that the organisational structure and programme content of the services must be such as to ensure their European character. In practice this requires that the services should be:

- independent of both national governmental influence and European institutional dominance;

- subject not to national broadcasting law but to the appropriate European statutes;

- multinational in character, orientation and staffing;

- independent of political or institutional control other than that of the European Court of Auditors.

The design of the management structure required to ensure that each service complies with these criteria will require detailed work at the time when the new services are created. We would hope that the European Television Forum, whose creation we recommend in Chapter 7, will undertake, in association with the promoters of the new services, the design of the necessary structures.

The most important element in any television service is its audience. In the development of the European public television services the need to ensure a reasonable number of viewers must therefore be paramount. At the same time as the European service needs viewers, the national public television services are increasingly in need of financial resources. It seems axiomatic to the Task Force that these complementary needs should, wherever possible, lead to the use by the national television services of the programmes which the European services can provide. This will ensure for the latter access to the substantial pre-existing audience of the national services; and for the former programmes made available at no additional cost to the subscribing national television services. Such arrangements will be particularly appropriate for a European News Service, such as is at present under discussion within the EBU.

Not all European public television services should be accommodated in the national services; the proposed high quality service should be able to attract significant minority shares of the European audience without difficulty, given appropriate transfrontier transmission and reception facilities. European households are generally prepared to invest in new media if the cost-benefit ratio is right. Reception of a European television service should therefore need only modest extra expenditure per household. In practice we would expect the equipment needed to receive channels to be part of the normal cable or Direct Broadcast Satellite reception equipment. It should be capable of receiving the European services in the local language and in the original language of the broadcast.

We conclude that both the need and the opportunity exist for the creation in the medium term of viable European television services in the public interest. Such services will not only contribute to the recognition by the people of Europe of their common heritage and their common future; they will serve to represent Europe to the rest of the world as they come to be transmitted by satellite to the Americas, to Africa, Asia and the Pacific. It is, in our view, no exaggeration to assert that the future health of Europe is linked with the future of its television services.

Chapter 7
A European television forum

The need for a new approach

As indicated in the first three chapters of this report, television in Europe is currently undergoing its first profound transformation since its establishment some thirty-five years ago. This transformation is characterised by a growing commercialisation and internationalisation, neither of which has in the past been a significant feature of the way that television has been organised in most European countries. Out of this transformation will emerge different economic structures for television services, and a different range of programmes offered to the viewers. We are already experiencing some of the consequences of these changes, particularly with regard to the fragmentation of audiences and the financial structures of television. Chapters 4 to 6 of this Report have explored some of the principal tasks ahead: the creation of a framework for competition; the maintenance of a strong audiovisual programme production industry; and the development of television services with a European dimension. The emergence of this new mood of competition and of transfrontier activities creates the need for a new regulatory framework within which the broadcasting industry can grow and flourish. The Task Force is of the opinion that the emerging broadcasting structures require such a new framework and new partnerships in which they can develop.

One of the most important tasks ahead will be the development of a formal framework for competition, discussed in Chapter 4. If an effective system can be established now on a voluntary basis, formal and constraining regulation at a later point will be unnecessary. If conflict and a ruthless ratings war are to be avoided, a "third way" has to be found. For this a meeting point has to be established to which all those involved in broadcasting have access.

Options for a Formal Framework

The European Television Task Force has considered at length a wide range of possible structures and mechanisms to meet the need for such a framework. It quickly became clear to us that there were two main possibilities to be considered:

● the creation of a statutory body with a formal mandate from institutions with the power to grant it, or

● the establishment of a non-governmental body.

The prime considerations in the search for a suitable framework are the need to maintain the independence of broadcasting from state intervention and to create an environment in which both public and private broadcasters can find breathing space for their development.

The statutory option: a European Broadcasting Authority

A European Broadcasting Authority could not be established by itself but only by legislation. Laws binding on the countries of Europe can derive only from:

● Legislation of the European Community, which is applicable only to Member States of the Community;

● Instruments of the Council of Europe which are applicable to Member States of the Council of Europe, and only insofar as they are ratified by each Member State;

● Treaties between States.

Under any of these methods it would, theoretically at least, be possible to establish a statutory body with defined powers. The evidence taken in the various hearings with experts from most European countries as well as the Task Force's own deliberations led to the conclusion that the statutory option was not feasible, at least at this stage. It seemed unlikely that the European Institutions would be able to establish legally binding instruments covering the necessary range of activities or to provide an infrastructure to administer them. Nor could we see a wide-ranging treaty being accepted within a reasonable time by a sufficient number of states.

A variant which we considered was a formal grouping of the various national regulatory agencies such as the IBA of the United Kingdom, the CNCL of France, the Media Raad of the Netherlands and the Konferenz der Landesmedienanstalten of the Federal Republic of Germany. Under this arrangement, the agencies would be expected collectively to draw up and enforce a charter of responsibilities for transfrontier broadcasters in Europe.The idea of a grouping of regulatory agencies was *prima facie* attractive to some members of the Task Force but we had to accept that, in any event, such agencies' jurisdiction was legally applicable only to national situations and also that regulatory agencies did not exist in any uniform way.

We decided therefore to proceed with the non-governmental option.

The Non-governmental Option: A European Television Forum

We recommend that a European Television Forum should be established as a non-governmental body with a membership representative of all the main interests concerned in the development of television in Europe. In the following pages we deal with the functions, the establishment, the structures and the membership of such a Forum.

The functions of the European Television Forum

The general function of the proposed European Television Forum would be the promotion of harmonious and coherent development of television in Europe. To this end, its first task would be to further the implementation of the recommendations contained in Chapter 8 of this Report, and to pursue the public and professional debate on the structure, content, quality and impact of transfrontier television in Europe.

More specifically, the work of the Forum would be grouped under the following main heads:

Policy and regulatory matters

The organisation of transfrontier broadcasting in Europe is very much an uncharted domain. The draft Directive of the Commission of the European Communities and the proposed Convention of the Council of Europe are of potential importance in securing the free flow of television programmes across frontiers. But it is difficult to foresee exactly how they will work in practice. There are those who believe that they will place undue obstacles in the way of the free development of the medium as it emerges from its regulated, nationally oriented, phase. Others tend to feel that insufficient emphasis is being placed on the maintenance of quality in what is available at the moment, and that action is being taken whose effects will be difficult to reverse. The two proposed instruments contain some provisions for monitoring their operation; (in the case of the Directive the main burden would, of course, fall on the Member States.) But these provisions are not very exacting and do not provide for any consistent participation in the monitoring process by professional broadcasters or viewers. These groups have a particular interest in how transfrontier broadcasting is developing and in the impact it is having at the national level.

It is clear that, whether independently or in some form of association with the European Institutions, all those involved in transfrontier television – broadcasters, producers, advertisers and consumers – ought to have the opportunity to appraise the working of these instruments, to identify problems and shortcomings in them and, if necessary, to suggest changes. They would be in a position to do so not as a lobby or pressure group but on the basis of expertise and experience.

An aspect of television policy not directly covered by the proposed Directive and Convention is that of the growth of multimedia groups and multipurpose television organisations with a number of functions – distribution, production and transmission, for instance – in the audiovisual field. There are also companies which have interests in audiovisual operations in a number of countries. The Task Force has made certain general recommendations in Chapter 2 designed to safeguard the public interest and the interests of broadcasting generally. But the issues raised will be of continuing relevance.

The above are examples of issues which call for a common international platform for discussion and, in certain areas, for the avoidance or resolution, of conflict. The need arises from the increased internationalisation and from the fact that the European Broadcasting Union does not include in its membership many transfrontier and private broadcasters. There is need, therefore, for a more widely constituted mechanism for discussion of programme trends and for the formulation of opinion about them. For example, the criticism expressed during the past year of certain journalistic trends, in broadcasting and in the press, could have benefitted from fuller public debate.

Advertising is of growing importance in the economy of television. Until recently there was a broad balance across Europe as a whole in the total amounts available to television from licence fees and from advertising. The balance is now changing; advertising revenue is growing and licence income is tending to stagnate. The number of television services dependent on advertising for their existence and for the capacity to produce programmes of quality will greatly increase in number. In so competitive a situation it is inevitable, as has been pointed out earlier in this report, that there will be an impact on the existing services. This has general implications for quality. Furthermore, the amount of advertising, the way in which it is inserted in the programmes, and its contents are themselves all factors affecting quality. These are all matters whose collective consideration is necessary in order to master the continuing internationalisation of television and the move towards a common European market by 1992.

The promotion of standards and quality in programmes

The Forum's activities in these fields would encompass the following:

- observation, discussion, and formulation of opinions about programme trends;

- stimulation of international training and staff exchange;

- providing a meeting point for all broadcasters (public, private, national and transfrontier), independent producers, advertisers, political decision makers, critics and viewers to discuss the purpose and content of television with a view to improving the quality of the programmes;

- consideration of ways in which European production can be stimulated and the circulation of programmes improved, with a particular eye being kept on the needs of the smaller organisations and countries.

An advantage of the Forum in the above areas would be the representation of the consumers among its members. This, coupled with the Forum's interest in audience research would enable producers to be made directly aware of, and it is hoped responsive to, public reaction to programmes and programme trends.

Operational and co-ordinating arrangements

There is a number of areas where a common approach, or the opportunity for discussion among all parties concerned, would be valuable. There are other fields where the provision of common services or the exercise of a co-ordinating role would lead to greater efficiency and economies of scale.

Under the heading of the need for a common approach we have in mind:

- **Copyright:** this is an area where divisions between different interests can be sharp and where a common meeting ground would be useful.

- **Political broadcasting:** most countries have their own rules to ensure fairness in the use of broadcasting by political parties, particularly at election times. Similar provisions are called for in transfrontier broadcasting to ensure that it is properly used for political purposes.

- **Access to major sporting and other events:** in a number of countries arrangements, formal or consensual, are in existence to prevent one broadcasting organisation gaining exclusive rights in events, sporting or otherwise, of such major importance that all organisations should have the opportunity to broadcast them if they so wish. The application of similar arrangements at the European level is a matter of continuing urgency.

Examples of areas where co-operation or joint initiatives would help are:

- **Transfrontier audience research:** This will more and more be required by both advertisers and broadcasters. Up to now highly sophisticated national audience research systems have existed in the different European countries, but they are mostly incompatible; nor do they normally take account of audiences reached outside the country concerned. There is the need to establish a Europe-wide compatible research mechanism which would command the confidence of the broadcasters, the advertisers and the public;

- **Language conversion:** Improvements in language conversion would reduce barriers to a wider international programme flow, with consequent advantage to all broadcasters (including those from the smaller countries) and the public alike. The European Institute for the Media's language project has identified the variety of approaches adopted and the different sets of facilities and operational teams active in sub-titling and dubbing.[1] There is a need for collective consideration by the Institute, the *MEDIA* initiative, the EBU and the professional bodies concerned of the possibility of co-ordination, standardisation and use of common facilities.

● **The assembly of data and statistics:** The creation and operation of a European programme data bank containing all the relevant information for programme sales and acquisitions has been called for repeatedly and is considered an urgent matter. Similarly, the assembly and evaluation of data and statistics concerning transfrontier broadcasting as well as further media research at a European level are essential to keep track of, and properly to understand, continuing developments.

● **International marketing and distribution:** Compared with those who provide English-language programmes, many European producers have to cope with a double market disadvantage: firstly, they have to recoup their production costs primarily in their own domestic market, in every case smaller than that of the United States; secondly, access to export markets is impeded by language and cultural barriers. Concerted efforts to overcome these problems are needed. They should include creation of a European data bank, conventional marketing methods such as catalogues, fairs, export shows etc., as well as co-operative sales initiatives. Success in these efforts could particularly benefit smaller independent producers.

● Running through all the suggested functions of the Forum is the need to undertake policy-oriented research. Using resources of the European Institute for the Media the Forum will be able to secure the information it requires to undertake work of practical value to broadcasters, public and private; politicians and viewers.

It is not suggested that the proposed European Television Forum would wish to take all possible activities under its wing at once. But there seems a need for a body, professionally expert and independent, to keep developments under constant review with

---

1   The European Institute for the Media: "Overcoming Language Barriers in European Television", Report, forthcoming (Autumn 1988) Manchester.

the possibility of suggesting, and arranging, such measures of co-ordination and standardisation as may be required by its members.

The establishment, composition and organisation of the European Television Forum

Establishment of the Forum

The Task Force urges that the European Cultural Foundation and the European Institute for the Media should, as soon as possible, establish the European Television Forum. We hope that the Foundation would enable the Institute to place at the disposal of the Forum its resources of documentation, information (including publications) and research.

The Composition, Financing and Organisation of the Forum

We see the Forum itself as consisting of between fifty and seventy persons of standing. It should however, be a main feature of the Forum to provide a meeting ground for all the main interests relevant to European broadcasting by the creation of specialist working groups whose membership would include the following:

- public and private broadcasters;

- advertising interests;

- consumer interests representing the viewers;

- trade union representation;

- film producers;

- television producers from outside the broadcasting organisations;

- academics concerned with media study and research;

- individuals of distinction appointed in their own right.

It will be important that there should be effective liaison between the Forum and the EBU, the EC and the Council of Europe, but it will be for later discussion whether this should be secured by membership of the Forum or by some other form of association.

The work of the Forum will need adequate financial support. While membership should be by personal appointment of specific individuals, it would be proper, in the case of those coming from organisations and companies, for those organisations to contribute to the support of the Forum.

The Forum as a whole will meet in full session once or twice a year. Its work will need the guidance of a small Executive Committee. We would expect the membership of the Executive Committee to be such as to secure continuity between its work and that which the Task Force has now completed. There should also be suitable cross-membership between the Executive Committee and the Council of the Institute.

Chapter 8
Summary and Recommendations

Chapter 1: Television in the Lives of the People

Summary

The importance of television in people's lives is no longer disputed: Europeans spend half their leisure time watching television. However much time is spent in front of it, television acts as a window opening out onto the whole world. For most people it is their main source of information and the strongest influence on the way they see world events. It also provides an unrivalled means of education and entertainment.

After a generation of relatively stable growth, television is now undergoing a more rapid phase of development. In the years to come, the majority of viewers will have a choice of between ten and twenty channels. These channels are likely to be less regulated but more international and commercial.

The European Television Task Force believes that this increase in television services could be a positive development in that it will increase the range of choice available to the viewer. Nevertheless, it is not without danger for the quality of the audiovisual system as a whole. The commercialisation of television could lead broadcasters to disregard their public and cultural responsibilities. Rather than improving the range of choices, the increase in the number of channels competing for the same audience could lead to a uniformly less ambitious programme output.

Recommendations

1.1. National and European authorities should guarantee the freedom of distribution and reception throughout Europe of all television services originated in Europe, to the extent that they conform to the law of the country of origin and that they comply with the relevant European Directives and Conventions.

1.2. Commercial aims, in particular income from advertising and sponsorship, must be subordinate to programme provision. Standards governing the amount, form and content of advertising material must be established at the European level. They must be applied under public control in the country of origin by all broadcasters.

1.3. All broadcasters, public and private, must be aware of their accountability to the audience to which their programmes are directed, whether at the national or the European level.

Chapter 2: The New Television Landscape

Summary

Changes in Broadcasting Technology

The development of cable, the use of telecommunication satellites for television, the imminent arrival of direct broadcast satellites and the possibilities of encryption all represent a degree of technical development which is changing the shape of television.

Common technical standards are necessary to achieve a common market for television. National governments and electronic industries have a tendency to develop their own standards for satellite transmission systems, cable distribution, teletext systems and encryption methods providing conditional access to the various forms of pay-TV. This is potentially harmful and there is a need instead to promote European co-operation in this field, as is currently the case in a Eureka project on high definition television which brings together manufacturers and broadcasters from various European countries.

The use of fixed satellite services has altered the traditional concept of television. The authorisation, in most European countries, for individuals to instal their own aerials to receive transmissions from these satellites raises questions of compatibility with the regulations laid down by the International Telecommunications Union (particularly RR 960). These regulations lay particular emphasis on the principle of such services being confidential to particular recipients and they therefore need to be adapted to correspond with what is actually happening.

Changes in Broadcast Structures

In the majority of European countries, the monopolies held by the national public service broadcasters in the fields of transmission, programming and production have either disappeared completely or are in the process of doing so. The principle of competition in broadcasting is establishing itself to varying degrees in different countries, making the industry more complex and its regulation more difficult.

The Task Force believes that a "third way" for European television should be found as soon as possible. The new organisational framework should not resemble the former public service monopoly system, nor should it take the form of uncontrolled competition which is practised elsewhere in the world. The quest for a harmonised system embracing both public service and private broadcasters and general and thematic channels should aim to safeguard the general level of quality which European television, with all its imperfections, has given as an example to the world.

In these circumstances, the formation of substantial media organisations to develop multimedia strategies on an international level may be a necessary development to enable the European programme industry to take its proper place in the world market. However, care will have to be taken to ensure that the process of concentration does not lead to abuse of dominant positions, as this would invalidate the principle of open competition and could threaten political pluralism and cultural diversity.

Changes in Audience Behaviour

The increase in the number of channels available, the growing use of video cassette recorders and the fact that many homes have several television sets, have led to a fragmentation of the audience. Viewing is done less collectively, programmes can be recorded and watched later, and viewers tend to be more ready to change channels: for example, they will quickly switch from one channel to another to avoid the advertisements ("zapping").

There is an increasing diversification in programming. In order to be able to offer advertisers particular audience exposure, broadcasters now compose their schedules around target audiences. This is particularly notable with "thematic channels" (variety, music, sport, films, children's TV, etc). But it is also evident in the so-called "general interest" channels which offer a wide variety of programmes.

Recommendations

2.1. The developing competition in the field of transfrontier television must be set in a European framework which allows for the co-existence of both public and private broadcasting organisations, whether offering general or thematic services. This framework should also encourage original production reflecting European identity in all its diversity.

2.2. Free competition among television services must be accompanied by arrangements to ensure the continuing existence and development of national audiovisual creativity, particularly in the smaller countries.

2.3. It is essential to ensure that concentration of ownership and control does not interfere either with freedom of competition or with freedom of expression. The safeguards provided by Articles 85 and 86 of the Treaty of Rome, together with those deriving from Article 10 of the European Convention on Human Rights, must be reinforced by provisions to deal with:

- the abuse of dominant positions in the media;

- the conditions of access to major events;

- the permissible limits of cross-ownership in the media.

2.4. It is also necessary to guard against such a multiplication of general channels that they are unable to attract sufficient resources to achieve high standards and reasonable programme origination.

2.5. It is recommended that a single common standard for satellite broadcasting, capable of being developed into a standard for high definition television should be adopted throughout Europe. European manufacturers should accelerate the marketing of television sets able to receive signals from terrestrial transmitters, satellites and cable systems.

2.6. A common, or at least compatible, system of encryption should be developed to allow the reception throughout Europe of conditional access television services. These services should come under legal protection, at European level, against unauthorised reception.

2.7. The opportunities presented by technological developments must be used to offer the peoples of Europe a wide range of services and programmes in the language of their choice.

Chapter 3: Quality in Television

Summary

The concept of quality in television is not easy to define. However, certain minimum requirements regarding technical matters and programme content must be met for a television station to be regarded as having attained an acceptable level of quality.

The Task Force is agreed that the notion of quality should not be confused with that of high cultural value. Furthermore, the pursuit of quality can as well be achieved by private broadcasters as by public service ones.

Advertising revenue is currently an indispensable part of the funding of television. Over the past decades, a mixed system of licence fees and advertising revenue has been adopted in most European countries. The private services, which will be an integral part of the new audiovisual landscape, will have to rely on advertising and sponsorship for their livelihood unless they provide subscription services.

The presence of advertising should not in itself be regarded as automatically detracting from programme quality. But an excessive amount, bad distribution and placement in the programmes, and harmful content and presentation are all factors which do detract from quality. There should be clearly defined standards on all these matters and about sponsorship (see also Recommendation 1.2)

Recommendations

3.1. A television service of high quality, whether general or thematic, should:

- respect human dignity and fundamental rights;

- respond to the interests of its audience, as well as presenting it with a wide view of the world at large and extending its horizons;

133

- include a substantial proportion of original material either produced or commissioned;

- produce its news programmes in a spirit of objectivity, independent of government or other interests;

- guarantee freedom of expression and encourage the free development of opinion reflective of the pluralist nature of society.

3.2. Broadcasting authorisations to public and private organisations, whether granted by national or European authorities, should require:

- professional competence;

- a sound financial base for their operations;

- a commitment to standards governing the content of programmes, in particular as regards racial discrimination, violence, taste and decency;

- compliance with current technical standards.

3.3. The public service broadcasting organisations must be assured of the resources necessary to provide and develop the full range of their services.

3.4. Terms and conditions should be applied to both national and transfrontier private broadcasters, taking into account the programme range they offer as well as the resources available to them, so as to ensure that all television organisations play an active part in audiovisual production.

3.5. The provisions of Article 6bis of the Berne Convention relative to the rights of authors should be reflected in national legislation in order to ensure respect for the integrity of artistic works, as well as in the interest of viewers.

Chapter 4: A European Framework for Competition

Summary

The possibility of transfrontier television, by means of satellite and or cable, gives rise to the need for a European regulatory framework. Sharing the same goal - the free circulation of television services throughout Europe — the Commission of the European Community and the Council of Europe are aiming to establish such a framework. The Commission is working on a draft Directive and the Council of Europe on a proposed Convention. The legal bases, the scope and the purport of these two texts, which are currently under discussion at ministerial level, are different. However, it is desirable that the content of the two documents should converge as much as possible.

Restrictive legislation also exists regarding technical matters (e.g. the International Telecommunication Union regulations and the recommendations of the European Conference on Post and Telecommunications Administration), as do standards of practice set by the professional organisations (eg the European Broadcasting Union, the International Chamber of Commerce and the European Advertising Tripartite).

These rules and regulations contribute — or will contribute — towards the creation of a European framework for broadcasting. However, individually they cannot guarantee the kind of coherent overall European broadcasting policy which is outlined in the 9th Declaration of the Board of Governors of the European Cultural Foundation of 30 May 1986 (see Annex 3).

Recommendations

4.1. It is recommended that there should be compatibility between the draft Directive of the Commission of the European Communities and the Council of Europe's proposed European Convention on broadcasting across frontiers. Furthermore it is recommended that they should be brought into force to the extent that the measures and provisions are in accord with the general intention of this Report.

4.2. The principle of quotas for European programmes and original production should be adopted, at least temporarily. Whether calculated on the total of all broadcast programmes or only on the total of drama, quotas should be applied to television services irrespective of their legal status or sources of finance.[1]

4.3. The proposed provisions of the draft Directive of the Commission of the European Communities that the promotion of audiovisual production and distribution should be extended to the Member States of the Council of Europe and EFTA on the basis of reciprocal agreements to be negotiated, should be adopted by Member States.

4.4. Legislation covering authors' rights and neighbouring rights should be reviewed and co-ordinated at the European level so as to allow artists, writers and performers to receive a fair share of the proceeds deriving from the expansion and internationalisation of broadcasting.

4.5. The proposal of the draft Directive of the European Communities to resolve the problems of copyrights in transfrontier television by negotiation among all interested parties (copyright organisations, producers, broadcasters and cable operators) and, in the absence of agreement, by arbitration in which the rights holders are represented, should be adopted by Member States.

4.6. It is desirable that the European Broadcasting Union (EBU) should include transfrontier broadcasters as members, in addition to the national broadcasters. In exchange for services offered by the EBU to these new members it should insist on the observance by them of the rules of professional conduct applicable to the existing EBU members.

Chapter 5: A Dynamic Television Programme Industry

Summary

The benefits which viewers can derive from the increase in the number of television channels available depend on the broadcasters' ability to offer a full and varied programme schedule. At the moment in Europe, although there has been a considerable

---

1   Dr Peter Schiwy and Sir Ian Trethowan dissent from any proposal to impose quotas. Rather than imposing protectionist measures they consider the recommendations made in Paragraphs 5.1 to 5.11 adequate so as to ensure the development of a dynamic television production industry in Europe.

increase in the number of programming hours, production is in a state of stagnation and in some areas, such as cinema films and television drama, it is actually decreasing. The frequent recourse to low budget programmes, repeats and imported programmes presents a serious threat to the quality of European television. European cultural identity is particularly at risk from the import of programmes from countries with advanced production technology such as the United States, Japan, Brazil and Australia. So too is Europe's trade balance: it is calculated that Europe's net deficit on the import and export of audiovisual programmes in 1986 was some 1 400 million ecu.

Europe is not lacking in creative talent or production capacity. In order to give them the chance to thrive, European and national authorities have an important role to play: they must take a series of measures of support, direct and indirect, to help the European audiovisual production industry.

Recommendations

5.1. Measures of support for the development of European audiovisual production are an essential complement to the application of provisions to ensure the free movement across borders of television services.

5.2. Such measures of support should cover not only the production and co-production of audiovisual material but also its promotion, distribution and broadcasting throughout Europe. The improvement of the technical, cultural and economic conditions applying to language transfer should be given high priority.

5.3. The activities of the European Commission, undertaken in the context of the MEDIA project and in association with the appropriate professional groups, covering production and broadcast of audiovisual works and cinema films should be adequately funded to ensure their satisfactory realisation and development.

5.4. Resolution No.1 on the promotion of the European audiovisual works, adopted at the First European Ministerial Conference on Mass Media Policy of the Council of Europe on 9 and 10 December 1986 in Vienna, should be implemented.

5.5. The co-operation agreed in principle between the European Commission and the Council of Europe to co-ordinate their activities for the encouragement of the audiovisual industry must be given effective form.

5.6. The European Broadcasting Union should develop its initiatives in the co-production and distribution of original audiovisual material, in the reduction of obstacles to multilingual programmes, and in the professional training of creative and production staff.

5.7. All European countries should take part in the multilateral support arrangements for the co-production of films and for the programme industries launched under the name EURIMAGES and enjoying the patronage of the Council of Europe.

5.8. Existing mechanisms of direct support for cinema production in different countries should be maintained and extended to cover independent audiovisual production. These support mechanisms should preferably be financed by means of levies on either or both of the hardware or software sales of the communications industries at large, rather than by subsidy from public funds which is of its nature uncertain.

5.9. The following fiscal measures should be taken where they do not already exist:

- the establishment of tax allowances for investments in the audiovisual programme industry;

- the creation of investment funds allowing small investors to provide capital for the audiovisual industry;

- the approximation of legal and fiscal provisions to encourage co-production between partners in the European countries;

- the application to the film and television industries of value added tax within an agreed reduced range of rates.

5.10. The financing of the film industry should be assured by the increased participation of television in film production, as well as by efforts to maintain satisfactory levels of cinema attendance to which the careful scheduling of films on television can contribute.

5.11. Smaller countries and regions in which the audiovisual production industry is least developed should receive priority in any arrangement for the support of audiovisual industries. It is also desirable that the European Regional Development Fund should in the future give special consideration to support for the cultural industries in such countries and regions.

Chapter 6: New European television services

Summary

There is already a number of television services in Europe whose survival depends on the existence of a European public, whose geographic distribution does not correspond to national frontiers. These channels are already using various possibilities offered by fixed service satellites, cable networks and the growing number of individuals with their own receiving equipment. They all have different charters, different means of finance and different objectives. These services may be provided by public service organisations or private broadcasting companies, and they may be funded by contributions from national channels, subsidies, advertising revenue, sponsorship or subscription. Their objectives range from the dissemination throughout Europe of programmes in a particular language (e.g. TV5, 3-SAT, Super Channel and RAI-Uno), through the provision of general entertainment programmes (e.g. Sky Channel), to the provision of thematic channels for specific audiences (e.g. Filmnet, Screen Sport, Arts Channel, MTV Europe etc).

In areas where it is possible to receive either these services or channels from neighbouring countries, some audience does exist even if it is only marginal only. It should be noted, however, that some broadcasters (e.g. CLT and the Fininvest Group) prefer to base their European strategy on the provision of different channels for the various linguistic groups in Europe.

None of these transfrontier channels provides a truly European programme service. Problems such as translation, cultural differences and copyright present serious obstacles to the creation of a truly European channel. However, real European channels are needed for political, cultural and economic reasons. From a political point of view, such channels would serve to promote the current process of European integration. From a cultural point of view, they would encourage programme exchanges, a better understanding and good neighbourly relations among Europeans. From an economic point of view, they could provide significant financial returns — especially in the case of thematic channels — as they would have access to a potential audience of 125 million homes and 350 million individuals.

Recommendations

6.1. Multilingual European television services working in the public interest should be established. These services should be primarily concerned with high quality programmes, drawing on the production resources of several countries as well as with a European news service.

6.2. A European news service could be operated as a specialised multilingual channel. Alternatively such a European news service should be progressively integrated in the general national or European television services.

6.3. The funding for such European services working in the public interest could come from national licence revenues, from national television organisations, and by direct grants from governments and/or European institutions.

Chapter 7. A European Television Forum

Summary

The new European television landscape requires new structures suitable to handle the issues posed by its internationalisation and growing commercialisation. Such structures could be built onto existing ones, or be created from scratch in accordance with the new requirements.

One of the most urgent needs is the creation of an effective organisation for handling harmonious competition which we have called the "third way". If the broadcasters themselves can establish such arrangements voluntarily, there will be less need for official regulation. As things stand, the creation of a European Television Authority does not appear possible at present, given the many national differences in this field. So the most feasible solution appears to be the creation of a forum for debate and interaction among the different elements in European television — a European Television Forum.

Recommendations

7.1. The evidence assembled in this Report has convinced the European Television Task Force of the need for a European body to promote the harmonious and coherent development of television in Europe.

7.2. Having considered a number of possible models for such a body, the Task Force recommends the establishment of a European Television Forum.

7.3. This Forum should be a non-governmental body whose membership should be representative of the main interests concerned with the development of European television.

7.4. The initial function of the Forum will be to promote the implementation of the recommendations made in this Report and to pursue the public and professional debate on the structure, content, quality and impact of transfrontier television in Europe.

Kapitel 8
Zusammenfassungen und Empfehlungen

Kapitel 1: Fernsehen im Leben der Menschen

Zusammenfassung

Die Bedeutung des Fernsehens im alltäglichen Leben der Menschen wird nicht mehr länger in Frage gestellt: die Europäer verbringen die Hälfte ihrer Freizeit damit, fernzusehen. Wieviel Zeit auch immer vor dem Apparat verbracht wird, Fernsehen ist ein Medium, das dem Zuhause ein Fenster in die ganze Welt eröffnet. Für die meisten Menschen ist es die Hauptinformationsquelle und nimmt starken Einfluss darauf, wie sie die Welt betrachten. Ebenso ist es ein bisher unerreichtes Medium zur Übermittlung von Bildung und Unterhaltung.

Nach einer Generation relativ stetiger Entwicklung befindet sich das Fernsehen nunmehr in einer Phase des Umbruchs. In den kommenden Jahren wird die Mehrheit der Zuschauer die Möglichkeit haben, zwischen 10 bis 20 Kanälen wählen zu können. Diese Kanäle werden aller Wahrscheinlichkeit nach weniger reguliert, aber internationaler und kommerzieller als das bisherige Fernsehen sein.

Die Initiativgruppe Europäisches Fernsehen ist der Überzeugung, dass das Anwachsen von Fernsehprogrammangebot eine positive Entwicklung insoweit ist, als damit die Auswahlmöglichkeiten, die dem Zuschauer zur Verfügung stehen, erweitert werden. Es ist dennoch nicht von der Hand zu weisen, dass diese Entwicklung nicht ohne Gefahren für die Qualität des gesamten audiovisuellen Systems ist. Die Kommerzialisierung des Fernsehens kann die Programmverantwortlichen dazu führen, ihre öffentliche und kulturelle Verantwortung ausser acht zu lassen. Anstatt die Auswahlmöglichkeiten zu verbessern, kann eine Kanalvielfalt, die miteinander im Wettbewerb um die gleiche Zuschauerschaft steht, auch zu immer einheitlicheren und weniger ehrgeizigen Programmproduktionen führen.

Empfehlungen

1.1. Die zuständigen nationalen und europäischen Behörden haben die freie Verbreitung und den ungehinderten Empfang aller Fernsehprogramme, die aus europäischen Ländern stammen, in Gesamteuropa sicherzustellen, sofern sie den Gesetzen des Ursprungslandes entsprechen und die einschlägigen Direktiven und Abkommen erfüllen.

1.2. Kommerzielle Ziele, insbesondere Erzielung von Gewinnen aus Werbung und Sponsoring, sind der Programmbeschaffung und -bereitstellung unterzuordnen. Normen, die Menge, Plazierung und Inhalte der Werbesendungen regeln, sind im europäischen Rahmen einzuführen. Diese Normen müssen für alle Fernsehveranstalter gelten, die in ihrem Sitzland der öffentlichen Aufsicht unterliegen.

1.3. Alle Fernsehveranstalter, ob öffentlich oder privat, müssen sich ihrer Verantwortung gegenüber dem nationalen oder europäischen Publikum, an das sich ihre Programme richten, bewusst sein.

Kapitel 2: Die neue Fernsehlandschaft

Zusammenfassung

Veränderungen in der Rundfunktechnik

Die technische Fortentwicklung von Breitbandkabel,Fernmeldesatelliten und direktempfangbaren Rundfunksatelliten (DBS) sowie die Möglichkeiten der Decodierung verändern auch die Gebrauchsformen des Fernsehens.

Allgemeingültige technische Normen sind notwendig, um einen gemeinsamen Fernsehmarkt in Europa aufzubauen. Die nationalen Regierungen der einzelnen Länder und die Elektronikindustrien neigen derzeit noch dazu, ihre eigenen Normen für Satellitenübertragungssysteme, Kabelverteilnetze, Teletextsysteme und Decodierungsmethoden für den Empfang verschlüsselter Pay-TV Sendungen zu entwickeln. Diese Tendenz kann möglicherweise ungewünschte Auswirkungen zur Folge haben, und es besteht desshalb die dringende Notwendigkeit, eine europäische Zusammenarbeit auf diesem Gebiet herbeizuführen. Dieses geschieht bereits im Rahmen eines Eureka-Projektes für ein hochauflösendes Fernsehen (HDTV), in dem Hersteller und Fernsehveranstalter aus verschiedenen europäischen Ländern zusammenarbeiten.

Die Nutzung von Fernmeldesatelliten hat das traditionelle Konzept von Fernsehen weitgehend verändert. Die Erteilung von Genehmigungen an Einzelpersonen zur Errichtung von Empfangsanlagen für Satellitensignale wirft in vielen Ländern die Frage nach der Kompatibilität mit den Bestimmungen, die von der Internationalen Fernmeldeunion ausgearbeitet wurden, besonders RR 960, auf. Diese Bestimmungen schützen besonders die Wahrung der Vertraulichkeit von Fernmeldediensten für die Empfänger, und es besteht daher die Notwendigkeit, sie den tatsächlichen Gegebenheiten anzupassen.

Veränderungen in den Strukturen des Fernsehens

In der Mehrzahl der europäischen Länder sind die bisherigen Monopolstellungen der öffentlich-rechtlichen Fernsehveranstalter auf dem Gebiet der Übertragung, Programmproduktion- und übermittlung bereits vollständig abgebaut oder weitgehend geschrumpft. Das Wettbewerbsprinzip fasst in diesem Sektor in unterschiedlichem Masse Fuss, und die Tatsache, dass die Fernsehlandschaft zunehmend verschachtelter wird, macht deren Kontrolle immer schwieriger.

Die Initiativgruppe ist der Überzeugung, dass ein "Dritter Weg" für das europäische Fernsehen so schnell wie möglich gefunden werden sollte. Dieser neue ordnungspolitische Rahmen sollte weder das bisherige öffentlich-rechtliche Monopolsystem festschreiben, noch sollte er einen völlig unkontrollierten Wettbewerb, wie er in anderen Teilen der Welt stattfindet, zulassen. Die Suche nach einem harmonischen System, das sowohl öffentlich-rechtliche als auch private Fernsehveranstalter sowie allgemeine und Spartenkanäle umfasst, sollte dem Leitziel folgen, dass das bisher erreichte Qualitätsniveau des europäischen Fernsehens, das trotz aller seiner Mängel als beispielhaft in der Welt gilt, nicht gesenkt wird.

Unter diesen Umständen mag die Herausbildung von grossen internationalen Medienkonzernen mit Weltmarktstrategien notwendig sein, damit die europäische Programmindustrie einen angemessenen Platz auf dem Weltmarkt einnehmen kann. Dabei muss allerdings dafür Sorge getragen werden, dass der damit verbundene Konzentrationsprozess nicht zu einem Missbrauch von marktbeherrschenden Positionen führt. Das würde das Prinzip des freien Wettbewerbs zunichte machen und den politischen Pluralismus sowie die kulturelle Vielfalt gefährden.

Veränderungen im Zuschauerverhalten

Kanalvielfalt, wachsende Videorecordernutzung und Haushalte, die mit mehr als einem Fernsehapparat ausgestattet sind, haben bereits zu einer Zersplitterung der Zuschauerschaft geführt. Immer weniger wird gemeinsam ferngesehen, da Sendungen aufgezeichnet und zu einem späteren Zeitpunkt wieder abgespielt werden können. Das Kanalspringen von einem zum anderen Kanal , auch um Werbespots zu umgehen ("zapping"), wird immer häufiger.

Zugleich ist eine zunehmende Programmspezialisierung festzustellen. Um den Werbekunden immer genauer definierte Zuschauergruppen anbieten zu können, gestalten Fernsehveranstalter ihre Programme zunehmend zielgruppenspezifisch. Besonders auffällig ist dies bei Spartenkanälen (Varieté, Musik, Sport, Film, Fernsehen für Kinder usw.), aber dieser Trend ist ebenso bei Vollprogrammen herkömmlicher Art zu verzeichnen.

Empfehlungen

2.1. Der sich entwickelnde Wettbewerb auf dem Gebiet des grenzüberschreitenden Fernsehens muss sich innerhalb einer europäischen Grundordnung abspielen, die das Nebeneinander von öffentlichen und privaten Fernsehorganisationen erlaubt, ob sie Voll-oder Spartenprogramme anbieten. Diese Grundordnung soll ausserdem Eigenproduktionen anregen, die die europäische Identität in all ihrer Vielfalt widerspiegeln.

2.2. Neben den freien Wettbewerb zwischen den Fernsehveranstaltern müssen Massnahmen treten, die den Fortbestand und die Entwicklung nationaler audiovisueller Kreativität sichern, besonders in den kleineren Ländern.

2.3. Es muss unbedingt sichergestellt werden, dass die Konzentration von Eigentum und Kontrolle weder den Wettbewerb noch die freie Meinungsäusserung beeinträchtigt. Die Garantien der Artikel 85 und 86 der Römischen Verträge und des Artikels 10 der Europäischen Menschenrechtskonvention müssen durch Regelungen abgesichert werden, die behandeln:

● den Missbrauch einer marktbeherrschenden Position in den Medien;

● die Zugangsbedingungen zu wichtigen Veranstaltungen;

● die Grenzen, innerhalb derer Doppelbesitz in den Medien geduldet werden kann.

2.4 Es ist ebenso notwendig, Massnahmen zu treffen, die eine unkontrollierte Zunahme von Fernsehkanälen verhindern. Eine solche Entwicklung könnte dazu führen, dass dann nicht mehr ausreichend finanzielle Mittel zur Verfügung stehen, um hohe Standards zu erreichen und angemessene Programme zu produzieren.

2.5. Es wird empfohlen, nur eine technische Norm für das Satellitenfernsehen in ganz Europa einzuführen, die zu einer Norm für hochauflösendes Fernsehen (HDTV) weiterentwickelt werden kann. Die europäischen Hersteller sollten den Vertrieb von solchen Fernsehgeräten vorantreiben, die in der Lage sind, Signale von allen terrestrischen Sendern, Satelliten und Kabelsystemen zu empfangen.

2.6. Ein allgemeines, zumindest kompatibles Decodierungssystem sollte entwickelt werden, das europaweit den Empfang verschlüsselter Fernsehprogramme möglich macht. Diese Programme sollten auf europäischer Ebene gesetzlich gegen unerlaubten Empfang geschützt werden.

2.7. Die Möglichkeiten, die sich durch neue technologische Entwicklungen ergeben, sollten dazu genutzt werden, den Menschen in Europa ein möglichst breites Angebot an Programmdiensten in der Sprache ihrer Wahl anzubieten.

Kapitel 3: Qualität im Fernsehen

Zusammenfassung

Qualität im Fernsehen ist nicht einfach zu definieren. Es müssen jedoch gewisse Mindestanforderungen, sowohl in technischer als auch in programmlicher Hinsicht erfüllt sein, damit ein Fernsehkanal ein akzeptables Qualitätsniveau erreicht.

Die Initiativgruppe hält fest, dass Qualität im Fernsehen nicht mit Kulturprogrammen gehobener Art verwechselt werden darf. Prinzipiell kann Qualität im Fernsehen von öffentlich-rechtlichen ebenso wie von privaten Fernsehveranstaltern erreicht werden.

Das Einkommen aus Werbung ist gegenwärtig ein unverzichtbarer Bestandteil der Finanzierung des Fernsehens. In den meisten europäischen Ländern wurden während der letzten Jahrzehnte Mischsysteme eingeführt, die Einkommen aus

Rundfunkgebühren und Werbung verbinden. Die privaten Fernsehveranstalter, die eine wesentliche Rolle in der neuen audiovisuellen Landschaft spielen, werden weiterhin vor allem auf Werbung und Sponsoring zu ihrer Finanzierung angewiesen sein, es sei denn, sie bieten ihre Programme im Abonnement an.

Das Vorhandensein von Werbung an sich sollte nicht automatisch als ein qualitätsminderndes Element im Programm angesehen werden. Werbung in übertriebenem Masse, sowie schlechte Verteilung und Plazierung im Programm, Inhalte und Darstellungen in verletzender Weise sind jedoch Faktoren, die qualitätsmindernd wirken können. Normen, die diese Elemente der Werbung, sowie das Problem des Sponsoring in einer klar definierten Weise regeln, sollten daher geschaffen werden (siehe auch Empfehlung 1.2).

Empfehlungen

3.1. Qualitätsprogramme im Fernsehen, ob Vollprogramme oder Spartenprogramme, sollten:

- die Würde und die Grundrechte der Menschen respektieren;

- auf die Bedürfnisse der Zuschauerschaft eingehen und ihr breitgefächerte Möglichkeiten der Weltsicht anbieten;

- einen wesentlichen Anteil von Eigen- oder Auftragsproduktionen enthalten;

- objektive Nachrichtensendungen produzieren und sie unabhängig von Regierungs- und anderen Interessen gestalten;

- die freie Meinungsäusserung garantieren, zur Entwicklung von eigenen Ansichten bei den Zuschauern beitragen und sich zum Pluralismus bekennen.

3.2. Sendelizenzen, die an öffentliche und private Organisationen durch nationale oder europäische Behördern erteilt werden, sollten voraussetzen:

- Professionalität und berufliche Fachkunde,

- eine gesicherte finanzielle Basis für den Betrieb;

- die Verpflichtung auf Normen, nach denen sich Programminhalte richten, insbesondere hinsichtlich Rassendiskriminierung, Gewalt, sowie gutem Geschmack und Moral;

- das Beachten der jeweils geltenden technischen Normen.

3.3. Den öffentlich-rechtlichen Rundfunkanstalten müssen die finanziellen Mittel garantiert werden, die sie benötigen, um ihrem Programmauftrag in seinem ganzen Umfang gerecht werden zu können.

3.4. Nationalen und grenzüberschreitenden privaten Fernsehveranstaltern sollten Pflichten bezüglich der Eigenprogrammproduktion auferlegt werden, wobei Programmangebotsart sowie die zur Verfügung stehenden Mittel zu berücksichtigen sind. Damit soll sichergestellt werden, dass sich alle Fernsehorganisationen aktiv an der audiovisuellen Produktion beteiligen.

3.5. Die Regelungen des Artikels 6bis der Berner Konvention hinsichtlich der Autorenrechte sollten in das nationale Recht integriert werden, um die Achtung vor der Integrität eines künstlerischen Werkes sicherzustellen und dem Interesse der Zuschauer zu dienen.

Kapitel 4: Eine europäische Grundordnung für den Wettbewerb

Zusammenfassung

Die Möglichkeit, grenzüberschreitendes Fernsehen mit Hilfe von Satelliten- oder Kabelsystemen zu verbreiten, macht eine europäische Fernsehgrundordnung notwendig. Sowohl die Kommission der Europäischen Gemeinschaften als auch der Europarat versuchen derzeit, eine solche Grundordnung auszuarbeiten und haben dabei das gleiche Ziel im Auge: die ungehinderte Verbreitung von Fernsehprogrammen in ganz Europa. Die Kommission hat einen Rahmenrichtlinienvorschlag und der Europarat einen Vorschlag für eine europäische Rundfunkkonvention vorgelegt. Die gesetzliche Grundlage, der Geltungsbereich und der Tenor beider Texte, die zur Zeit auf Ministerialebene diskutiert werden, sind jedoch unterschiedlich. Es ist demnach erforderlich, dass beide Dokumente so deckungsgleich wie möglich gemacht werden.

Ferner besteht eine separate Gesetzgebung auf technischem Gebiet (z.B. durch die Regeln der Internationalen Fernmeldeunion und die Empfehlungen der Europäischen Post- und Fernmeldeverwaltungskonferenz). In ähnlicher Weise wirken die praktischen Verfahrensregeln, aufgestellt von den berufsständischen Organisationen (z.B. der Europäischen Rundfunkunion, der Internationalen Industrie-und Handelskammer und der "European Advertising Tripartite").

All diese Regeln und Richtlinien tragen somit zur Herausbildung einer europäischen Grundordnung für den grenzüberschreitenden Rundfunk bei — oder werden es in der Zukunft tun. In ihrer Gesamtheit sind sie jedoch noch nicht dazu geeignet, eine kohärente gesamteuropäische Rundfunkordnung zu garantieren, so wie sie in der "Neunten Erklärung der Europäischen Kulturstiftung vom 30. Mai 1986" gefordert wurde (siehe Anhang).

Empfehlungen

4.1. Es wird empfohlen, Kompatibilität zwischen dem Rahmenrichtlinienvorschlag der Kommission der Europäischen Gemeinschaften und der vom Europarat vorgeschlagenen Europäischen Rundfunkkonvention für grenzüberschreitendes Fernsehen herzustellen. Weiter wird empfohlen, dass die Massnahmen und Bestimmungen derart in Kraft gesetzt werden, dass sie der allgemeinen Tendenz dieses Berichtes entsprechen.

4.2. Ein Quotenprinzip für die Ausstrahlung europäischer Programme und von Eigenproduktionen sollte — wenigstens vorübergehend — eingeführt werden. Dies sollte unabhängig davon geschehen, ob sich die Berechnung der Quoten auf alle Fernsehprogramme oder nur auf Sendungen mit Spielhandlung bezieht. Diese Quoten sollten auf die Programme aller Fernsehveranstalter zutreffen, gleichgültig, welchen rechtlichen Status sie haben oder wie sie finanziert werden.[1]

4.3. Die Mitgliedstaaten der EG sollten die in dem Rahmenrichtlinienentwurf der Kommission der Europäischen Gemeinschaften enthaltenen Vorschläge zur

---

[1] Sir Ian Trethowan und Peter Schiwy treten jeglicher Quotenregelung entgegen. Statt solcher Schutzmassnahmen sehen sie die Empfehlungen 5.1. — 5.10 dieses Reports als hinreichend an, um die Entwicklung einer dynamischen europäischen Fernsehindustrie sicherzustellen.

Ausweitung der Förderung audiovisueller Produktionen und deren Vertrieb auch auf die Mitgliedstaaten des Europarates und der EFTA auf der Basis gegenseitiger, noch abzuschliessender Abkommen, annehmen.

4.4. Die Gesetze, die die Urheberrechte und angrenzende Rechte behandeln, sollten überarbeitet und auf europäischer Ebene koordiniert werden, um sicherzustellen, dass Schriftsteller sowie schaffende und ausführende Künstler einen angemessenen Anteil der Einnahmen erhalten, die mit der Ausweitung und Internationalisierung von Fernsehprogrammen erzielt werden.

4.5. Der Vorschlag in den Rahmenrichtlinien der Kommission der Europäischen Gemeinschaft, der die Lösung von Urheberrechtsproblemen durch Verhandlungen zwischen allen betroffenen Parteien (Urheberrechtsorganisationen, Produzenten, Rundfunk- und Kabelveranstaltern) und, im Falle der Nichteinigung, durch ein Schiedsverfahren, bei dem alle Rechteinhaber vertreten sind, behandelt, sollte von den Mitgliedstaaten der EG angenommen werden.

4.6. Es wird empfohlen, dass die Europäische Rundfunkunion (EBU) neben den nationalen Rundfunkorganisationen auch grenzüberschreitende Rundfunkveranstalter als Mitglieder aufnimmt. Als Gegenleistung für die Dienste, die die EBU den neuen Mitgliedern zur Verfügung stellt, sollten diese sich zur Einhaltung der berufsständischen Verhaltensregeln bereitfinden, die für die nationalen EBU Mitglieder gelten.

Kapitel 5: Eine dynamische Fernsehprogrammindustrie

Zusammenfassung

Die Vorteile, die sich für den Zuschauer aus einer wachsenden Fernsehprogrammvielzahl ergeben, hängen letzlich davon ab, inwieweit die Fernsehveranstalter in der Lage sind, ein umfassendes und abwechslungsreiches Programm anzubieten. Zur Zeit stagniert die Programmproduktion in Europa im Falle von Kino- und Spielfilmen, obgleich ein beachtlicher Anstieg in den Fernsehsendezeiten zu vermerken ist. Zunehmende Seundungswiederholungen, Billigproduktionen und Importprogramme stellen auf lange Sicht eine ernstzunehmende Gefahr für die Qualität im europäischen Fernsehen dar. Die kulturelle Identiät Europas ist besonders gefährdet durch den Import von Sendungen aus Ländern mit fortschrittlicher Produktionstechnik, wie z.B. aus den Vereinigten Staaten, Japan, Brasilien und Australien. Parallel zu überproportionalen Programmimporten gerät die audiovisuelle Handelsbilanz

Europas aus dem Gleichgewicht: das Nettodefizit Europas bei der Ein-und Ausfuhr von Film-und Fernsehprogrammen lag im Jahre 1986 bei etwa 1,4 Milliarden Ecu.

In Europa fehlt es nicht an kreativem Talent oder Produktionskapazitäten. Deshalb spielen europäische und nationale Behörden eine wichtige Rolle, wenn es darum geht, der Produktionsindustrie eine Chance für eine erfolgreiche Entwicklung zu geben. Sie müssen eine Reihe von Unterstützungsmassnahmen treffen, seien es direkte oder indirekte, um der europäischen audiovisuellen Produktionsindustrie zu einer angemessenen Position zu verhelfen.

Empfehlungen

5.1. Um die Bestimmungen über die freie Verbreitung von grenzüberschreitendem Fernsehen zu ergänzen, sind Massnahmen zur Förderung der Entwicklung europäischer audiovisueller Produktionen unbedingt notwendig.

5.2. Solche Förderungsmassnahmen sollten sich nicht nur auf Produktion und Koproduktion von audiovisuellem Material beziehen, sondern auch für das Marketing, den Vertrieb und die Ausstrahlung von Programmen überall in Europa gelten. Eine besonders grosse Bedeutung kommt dabei der Verbesserung der technischen, kulturellen und ökonomischen Bedingungen der sprachlichen Fernsehprogrammübersetzung zu.

5.3. Die Aktivitäten der Europäischen Kommission im Rahmen des MEDIA-Projekts, betrieben in Zusammenarbeit mit den Berufsverbänden, die für die Herstellung und Ausstrahlung von audiovisuellen Werken und Kinofilmen zuständig sind, sollten ausreichend finanziert werden, um eine zufriedenstellende Entwicklung und praktische Umsetzung sicherzustellen.

5.4. Die Resolution Nr. 1 über die Förderung von europäischen audiovisuellen Werken, angenommen von der Ersten Europäischen Ministerkonferenz des Europarates über Massenmedienpolitik am 9. und 10. Dezember 1986 in Wien, sollte in die Praxis umgesetzt werden.

5.5. Die Zusammenarbeit zwischen der Europäischen Kommission und dem Europarat, über die im Grundsatz Einigkeit besteht, muss verwirklicht werden, um deren Bemühungen zur Förderung der audiovisuellen Industrie miteinander in Einklang zu bringen.

5.6. Die Europäische Rundfunkunion sollte ihre Initiativen hinsichtlich der Koproduktion und Verbreitung von audiovisuellem Eigenmaterial, zum Abbau von Hindernissen für mehrsprachige Programme und zur beruflichen Aus-und Fortbildung der Beschäftigten im kreativen und produktiven Bereich verstärken.

5.7. Alle europäischen Länder sollten sich an den multilateralen Abkommen, die unter dem Namen EURIMAGES ins Leben gerufen wurden und sich der Schirmherrschaft des Europarates erfreuen, beteiligen.

5.8. Bestehende Systeme zur direkten Förderung von Film- und Fernsehproduktionen in den einzelnen Ländern sollten beibehalten und so erweitert werden, dass sie auch freien Produzenten zugänglich sind. Die Finanzierung dieser Förderungssysteme sollte vorzugsweise durch Abgaben auf die Soft- und/oder Hardwareerlöse der Kommunikationsindustrie geschehen und nicht durch Zahlungen aus öffentlichen Mitteln, die ihrer Natur nach unbeständig sind.

5.9. Die folgenden steuerlichen Massnahmen sollten eingeführt werden, wo sie nicht schon bestehen:

- die Gewährung von Steuervergünstigungen für Investitionen in die audiovisuelle Industrie;

- die Schaffung von Investitionsfonds, die es kleineren Anlegern ermöglichen, Kapital für die audiovisuelle Industrie bereitzustellen;

- die Angleichung von gesetzlichen und steuerlichen Bestimmungen, um Koproduktionen zwischen Partnern aus verschiedenen europäischen Ländern zu ermutigen;

- die Besteuerung der Film-und Fernsehindustrie mit einer ermässigten Mehrwertsteuer, deren Höhe innerhalb vereinbarter Ober-und Untergrenzen liegt.

5.10. Die zunehmende Beteiligung von Fernsehunternehmen an der Produktion von Filmen, sowie Bemühungen, dem Kino eine zufriedenstellende Zahl von Besuchern zu erhalten, sind zur Sicherung der Finanzierung der Filmindustrie notwendig. Ein massvoller Programmeinsatz der Filme im Fernsehen kann diesem Zweck dienen.

5.11. Kleinere Länder oder Regionen, in denen die audiovisuelle Programmindustrie am geringsten entwickelt ist, sollten Priorität bei der Förderung der audiovisuellen Industrie erfahren. Der *Europäische Regionale Entwicklungsfonds* sollte ebenfalls erwägen, Mittel für die Unterstützung der kulturellen Industrien in diesen Ländern und Regionen zur Verfügung zu stellen.

Kapitel 6: Neue europäische Fernsehprogrammdienste

Zusammenfassung

Es gibt bereits eine Anzahl von Fernsehstationen in Europa, die davon abhängen, ein europäisches Publikum zu erreichen, dessen geographische Verteilung nicht an Ländergrenzen gebunden ist. Diese Kanäle machen Gebrauch von den verschiedenen transnationalen Programm-, Sende- und Verbreitungsmöglichkeiten, die durch Fernmeldesatelliten, Kabelnetze und private Satellitenempfangseinrichtungen geboten werden. Sie alle haben unterschiedliche Satzungen, Wege der Finanzierung und Ziele. Es handelt sich dabei entweder um Ableger öffentlicher oder privater Rundfunkanstalten, oder aber um Kanäle, die durch Beiträge der nationalen Programme, Subventionen, Werbeeinnahmen, Sponsoring oder Subskription finanziert werden. Ihre Ziele reichen von der Verbreitung von Programmen in einem bestimmten Sprachraum Europas (z.B. TV 5, 3-SAT, Super Channel und RAI-UNO) bis zum Angebot allgemeiner Unterhaltungsprogramme (z.B. Sky Channel) oder der Bereitstellung von Spartenkanälen für ein spezifisches Publikum (z.B. Filmnet, Screen Sport, Arts Channel, MTV Europe usw.).

Grenzüberschreitende Overspill-Programme werden von einem Teil der nachbarstaatlichen Zuschauer in der Regel interessiert, aber nur in geringem Masse aufgenommen. Indessen sind einige internationale Fernsehanbieter (vor allem CLT, und die Fininvest Gruppe) dazu übergegangen, ihre Programmstrategie auf der Bereitstellung von verschiedenen Kanälen in den europäischen Hauptsprachräumen aufzubauen.

Keiner der bestehenden grenzüberschreitenden Kanäle bietet jedoch ein wirklich europäisches Programm an. Probleme, wie die der Programmübersetzung, kultureller Unterschiede und des Urheberrechts stellen ernsthafte Behinderungen bei der Schaffung eines wirklich europäischen Kanals dar. Wie dem auch sei, europäische Kanäle als solche werden schon allein aus politischen, kulturellen und ökonomischen

Gründen benötigt. Vom politischen Gesichtspunkt aus gesehen können solche Kanäle den gegenwärtigen europäischen Integrationsprozess fördern. Vom kulturellen Standpunkt aus gesehen, würden sie den Austausch von Sendungen anregen, sowie ein besseres Verständnis und gute nachbarschaftliche Beziehungen unter den Europäern schaffen helfen. Vom ökonomischen Gesichtspunkt aus gesehen könnten sie mit einem potentiellen Publikum von 125 Millionen Haushalten und 350 Millionen Einzelpersonen beträchtliche finanzielle Gewinne einbringen, besonders im Falle von Spartenkanälen.

Empfehlungen

6.1. Europäische Fernsehprogramme, die mehrsprachig sind und dem öffentlichen Interesse dienen, sollten geschaffen werden. Diese Rundfunkdienste sollten in erster Linie bemüht sein um:

● die Produktion von Qualitätsprogrammen, die auf die zur Verfügung stehenden Produktionskapazitäten in mehreren Ländern zurückgreifen können;

● einen europäischen Nachrichtendienst.

6.2. Ein europäischer Nachrichtendienst sollte als mehrsprachiger Kanal betrieben werden, der den Interessen unterschiedlicher Sprachgruppen dient. Als Alternative dazu könnten europäische Nachrichten zunehmend in die allgemeinen nationalen Fernsehprogramme integriert werden.

6.3. Europäische Rundfunkdienste, die dem öffentlichen Interesse dienen, könnten durch nationale Rundfunkgebühren, von nationalen Fernsehorganisationen oder durch direkte Subventionen seitens der Regierungen und/oder der Europäischen Institutionen finanziert werden.

Kapitel 7: Ein Europäisches Fernsehforum

Zusammenfassung

Die neue europäische Fernsehlandschaft erfordert neue Strukturen, die der gegenwärtigen Internationalisierung und wachsenden Kommerzialisierung des Fernsehens entsprechen. Solche neuen Strukturen können entweder auf bereits bestehenden aufgebaut, oder aber, unter Berücksichtigung neuer Erfordernisse, völlig neu geschaffen werden.

Eine der dringendsten Notwendigkeiten ist die Schaffung einer effektiven Organisation, die in der Lage ist, den von uns geforderten "Dritten Weg" eines harmonischen Fernsehwettbewerbs in Europa in die Praxis umzusetzen. Je eher und je freiwilliger entsprechende Vereinbarungen unter den Fernsehveranstaltern selbst getroffen werden können, desto weniger erforderlich werden staatliche Vorschriften und Regelungen zu einem späteren Zeitpunkt sein. Bei jetzigem Stand der Dinge scheint die Einrichtung einer "Europäischen Fernsehbehörde" nicht möglich, da noch zu viele nationale Unterschiede auf diesem Gebiet bestehen. Deshalb scheint uns die beste Antwort in der Gründung eines Forums zu liegen, in dem allle am Fernsehen in Europa beteiligten Interessen vertreten sind: – dem "Europäischen Fernsehforum".

Empfehlungen

7.1. Die in diesem Bericht zutage getretene Sachlage hat die Initiativgruppe Europäisches Fernsehen davon überzeugt, dass die Schaffung einer europäischen Einrichtung notwendig ist, um eine harmonisch aufeinander bezogene Entwicklung des Fernsehens in Europa zu fördern.

7.2. Nach umfassender Prüfung einer Reihe von möglichen Modellen für eine solche Einrichtung empfiehlt die Initiativgruppe die Schaffung eines Europäischen Fernsehforums.

7.3. Dieses Forum soll eine regierungsunabhängige Einrichtung sein, deren Mitglieder die wesentlichsten Interessensbereiche der Entwicklung des Fernsehens in Europa vertreten.

7.4. Zu Anfang wird es die Aufgabe des Forums sein, die Umsetzung der Empfehlungen dieses Berichtes voranzutreiben und öffentliche sowie Fachdiskussionen über Strukturen, Inhalte, Qualität und Auswirkungen von grenzüberschreitendem Fernsehen in Europa anzuregen.

Hoofdstuk 8
Samenvatting en Aanbevelingen

Hoofdstuk 1. Televisie in het dagelijks leven

Samenvatting

Dat de televisie een belangrijke plaats inneemt in het dagelijks leven van de mensen staat niet langer ter discussie: Europeanen besteden de helft van hun vrije tijd aan televisiekijken. Hoeveel tijd men ook voor het toestel doorbrengt, de televisie vormt een 'open raam' naar de wereld. Voor de meeste mensen is zij de voornaamste bron van informatie, met een zeer sterke invloed op hun manier van denken over gebeurtenissen in de wereld. De televisie verschaft ook een unieke vorm van educatie en amusement.

Na een periode van relatief stabiele groei, bevindt de televisie zich nu in een snellere ontwikkelingsfase. De meerderheid van de kijkers zal in de komende jaren de keuze hebben uit tien tot twintig netten. Deze netten zullen waarschijnlijk aan minder regels gebonden maar meer internationaal en commercieel van karakter zijn.

De *European Television Task Force* is van mening dat deze toename van het aantal te ontvangen netten positief kan zijn, inzoverre het de keuzemogelijkheid van de kijker vergroot. Toch zou deze ontwikkeling de kwaliteit van het audiovisuele systeem kunnen ondermijnen. De commercialisering van de televisie zou de omroepinstellingen ertoe kunnen brengen hun maatschappelijke en culturele verantwoordelijkheden te negeren. In plaats van het aantal keuzemogelijkheden uit te breiden zou de toename van het aantal netten dat zich op eenzelfde publiek richt, over de hele linie juist een daling in de kwaliteit van de programma's kunnen veroorzaken.

Aanbevelingen

1.1. De nationale en Europese overheden dienen de vrijheid van distributie en ontvangst in Europa van alle televisienetten van Europese oorsprong te garanderen, voor zover dit aanbod in overeenstemming is met de wetgeving van het uitzendende land en voldoet aan de voorwaarden neergelegd in de van toepassing zijndc Europese richtlijnen en conventies.

1.2. Commerciële doeleinden, met name inkomsten uit reclame en sponsoring, moeten ondergeschikt zijn aan het programma-aanbod. Normen met betrekking tot de hoeveelheid, vorm en inhoud van reclame moeten vastgesteld worden op Europees niveau. Deze normen moeten door alle omroepinstellingen toegepast worden en onderworpen zijn aan wettelijke controle in het uitzendende land.

1.3. Alle omroepinstellingen, publieke en commerciële, moeten zich bewust zijn van hun verantwoordelijkheden ten opzichte van het nationale of Europese kijkerspubliek tot wie zij hun programma's richten.

Hoofdstuk 2. Het nieuwe televisie landschap

Samenvatting

Veranderingen in de omroep-technologie

De gedaante van televisie wordt momenteel veranderd door een aantal technologische ontwikkelingen, zoals de uitbreiding van de kabel, het gebruik van telecommunicatie-satellieten door omroepinstellingen, binnenkort ook het bestaan van 'direct broadcasting satellites', en de mogelijkheden geboden door coderingstechnieken.

Standaardisering van de technische normen is noodzakelijk om een gemeenschappelijke markt voor televisie te kunnen vormen. Nationale regeringen en industriën neigen ertoe hun eigen technische normen te ontwikkelen voor satelliet transmissie, kabel distributie, teletext systemen en coderings-methoden voor toegang tot de verschillende vormen van betaal-televisie. Dit is mogelijk een gevaarlijke tendens en Europese samenwerking op dit gebied moet gestimuleerd worden, zoals momenteel het geval is in het kader van het *EUREKA* project over 'high definition television', dat fabrikanten en omroepinstellingen uit verschillende Europese landen samenbrengt.

Het gebruik van 'fixed satellite services' heeft het traditionele concept van televisie veranderd. De toestemming die in de meeste Europese landen aan particulieren gegeven wordt hun eigen schotel te installeren om satelliet-zenders te ontvangen, doet de vraag rijzen of dit wel overeenkomt met de bepalingen van de *International Telecommunication Union* (in het bijzonder RR 960). Deze bepalingen benadrukken met name het principe van vertrouwelijkheid van de zenders voor bepaalde ontvangers en moeten dus aangepast worden aan de praktijk.

Veranderingen in de omroep-structuren

In de meeste Europese landen is het monopolie van de binnenlandse publieke omroepen op het gebied van transmissie, programmering en productie volledig verdwenen, of bezig te verdwijnen. Concurrentie krijgt in meer of mindere mate voet aan de grond in deze sector. Het omroep-systeem wordt gekarakteriseerd door een groeiende complexiteit, wat regulering ervan moeilijker maakt.

De Task Force is van mening dat zo snel mogelijk een 'derde weg' voor Europese televisie gevonden moet worden. Zo'n nieuw kader moet niet lijken op de oude situatie van monopolie voor publieke omroepen, of resulteren in het soort ongecontroleerde concurrentie dat elders plaatsvindt. Het zoeken naar een systeem waarin publieke en commerciële netten van algemene en thematische aard naast elkaar bestaan, zou tot gevolg moeten hebben dat het kwaliteitsniveau, dat de Europese televisie, met al haar onvolmaaktheden, de wereld geboden heeft, bewaard wordt.

In deze omstandigheden kan het nodig zijn aanzienlijke media-organisaties op te richten om multimedia strategieën op internationaal niveau te ontwikkelen, met als doel de Europese programma-industrie de kans te geven een geschikte plaats op de wereldmarkt te verwerven. Echter, men zal er op toe moeten zien dat het proces van concentratie niet leidt tot misbruik van machtsposities, daar dit het principe van vrije concurrentie zou ontkrachten en een bedreiging zou kunnen vormen voor politieke en culturele pluriformiteit.

Veranderingen in het kijkersgedrag

De toename van het aantal te ontvangen netten, de groeiende populariteit van videorecorders en het feit dat vele huishoudens beschikken over verscheidene televisietoestellen heeft geleid tot een versnippering van het kijkerspubliek. Er wordt minder gezamenlijk gekeken, programma's kunnen opgenomen en later bekeken worden en kijkers hebben de neiging gemakkelijker van net te veranderen: ze zullen bijvoorbeeld snel van het ene net naar het andere overschakelen om reclame te vermijden ('zapping').

Er is een groeiende diversificatie in programmering. De netten richten hun programma-schema's in rond doelgroepen, om adverteerders een bepaalde groep van het publiek aan te kunnen bieden. Dit is bijzonder duidelijk in het geval van thematische netten (amusement, muziek, sport, films, netten voor kinderen, enz.). Maar dit doet zich ook voor bij de algemene netten, die een breed scala aan programma's aanbieden.

Aanbevelingen

2.1. De zich ontwikkelende concurrentie op het gebied van grensoverschrijdende omroep dient plaats te vinden binnen een Europees kader dat het mogelijk moet maken voor publieke en commerciële omroepinstellingen naast elkaar te bestaan, of ze nu een algemeen of thematisch programma uitzenden. Binnen dit kader zou ook de eigen productie, die de diversiteit van de Europese identiteit weergeeft, moeten worden bevorderd.

2.2. Vrije concurrentie tussen omroepinstellingen moet gepaard gaan met voorzieningen die het voortbestaan en de verdere ontwikkeling garanderen van de nationale creativiteit op audiovisueel gebied, met name in de kleinere landen.

2.3. Het is van essentieel belang er op toe te zien dat concentratie van bezit en controle noch nadelige invloed heeft op de vrije concurrentie noch op de vrijheid van meningsuiting. De garanties die geboden worden in de artikelen 85 en 86 van het Verdrag van Rome, tesamen met de garanties die voortvloeien uit artikel 10 van het Europees Verdrag voor de Rechten van de Mens, moeten worden versterkt met specifieke wettelijke bepalingen ten aanzien van:

● misbruik van dominante posities in de media-sector

● toelatingsvoorwaarden voor belangrijke evenementen

● toelaatbare grenzen voor vormen van concentratie en centralisatie in de media-sector.

2.4. Men dient eveneens op te passen voor een zodanige toename van algemene netten dat deze niet meer in staat zijn de nodige middelen aan te trekken om een hoog niveau te bereiken en een redelijke herkomst van programma's te verzekeren.

2.5. Aanbevolen wordt dat in heel Europa een gemeenschappelijke norm wordt vastgesteld voor omroep via satelliet, die kan worden ontwikkeld tot een norm voor 'high definition television'. De Europese industrie moet de productie van televisietoestellen, geschikt voor de ontvangst van aardse netwerken, satelliet en kabel, versnellen.

2.6. Een gemeenschappelijk, of tenminste compatibel, systeem voor codering moet worden ontwikkeld met het doel in heel Europa de ontvangst mogelijk te maken van vormen van betaal-televisie. Deze vorm van omroep moet op Europees niveau onder wettelijke bescherming komen te staan, om ongeoorloofde ontvangst tegen te gaan.

2.7. De mogelijkheden die geboden worden door de technische ontwikkelingen moeten aangewend worden om het Europese publiek een waaier van uiteenlopende netten en programmas aan te kunnen bieden in de taal van hun keuze.

Hoofdstuk 3. Kwaliteitstelevisie

Samenvatting

Het begrip kwaliteitstelevisie is moeilijk te definiëren. Toch moet een televisienet voldoen aan bepaalde minimum-eisen met betrekking tot technische zaken en programma-inhoud alvorens men ervan uit kan gaan dat zo'n net een aanvaardbaar kwaliteitsniveau heeft bereikt.

De Task Force is het erover eens dat het begrip kwaliteit niet verward moet worden met 'hoge culturele waarde'. Bovendien kan het streven naar kwaliteit even goed een zaak zijn van commerciële zenders als van publieke omroepen.

Reclame-inkomsten vormen tegenwoordig een onmisbaar onderdeel van de financiering van televisie. De meeste Europese landen hebben in de loop van de laatste decennia gekozen voor een gemengd systeem van inkomsten uit kijk-en luistergelden en reclame. De commerciële netten , die een volledig onderdeel zullen zijn van het nieuwe televisie-landschap, zullen voor hun voortbestaan afhankelijk zijn van reclame en sponsoring, tenzij ze abonnee-netten verzorgen.

De aanwezigheid van reclame moet op zichzelf niet beschouwd worden als schadelijk voor de kwaliteit van een programma. Echter een overdreven hoeveelheid, slechte verdeling en plaatsing in programma's, evenals schadelijke inhoud en presentatie zijn factoren die afbreuk doen aan die kwaliteit. Er zouden duidelijk omschreven normen moeten bestaan ten aanzien van al deze zaken en ten aanzien van sponsoring (zie ook Aanbeveling 1.2).

Aanbevelingen

3.1. Een kwalitatief hoogstaande omroep van algemene of thematische aard moet:

- de menselijke waardigheid en de fundamentele rechten van anderen respecteren;

- beantwoorden aan de behoeften en interesses van het publiek, hen een brede kijk op de wereld aanbieden en hun horizonten verruimen;

- een wezenlijk aandeel zelf of in opdracht geproduceerd materiaal bevatten;

- nieuwsuitzendingen maken in een geest van objectiviteit onafhankelijk van regerings- of andere invloeden;

- vrijheid van meningsuiting garanderen en vrije meningsvorming stimuleren in een geest van verscheidenheid als afspiegeling van de samenleving.

3.2. Aan zendmachtigingen voor publieke en commerciële omroepinstellingen, of ze nu verleend zijn door nationale of Europese overheden, moeten de volgende eisen worden gesteld:

- professionaliteit;

- een gezonde financiële basis voor de activiteiten;

● het in acht nemen van normen ten aanzien van de programma-inhoud, met name waar het gaat om rassendiscriminatie, geweld, en goede zeden;

● het zich verplichten tot naleving van de geldende technische normen.

3.3. De publieke omroepinstellingen moeten verzekerd zijn van de nodige financiële middelen om hun volledig programma aan te kunnen bieden en te ontwikkelen.

3.4. Uitgaande van de aard van de programma's en de omvang van de inkomsten moeten productievoorwaarden en programma-eisen worden opgelegd aan nationale en grensoverschrijdende omroepinstellingen, zulks om te verzekeren dat zij een actieve rol spelen in de audiovisuele productie.

3.5. De bepalingen in artikel 6bis van de Conventie van Bern ten aanzien van de auteursrechten, moeten weerspiegeld worden in de nationale wetgeving van de Europese landen, om respect voor de integriteit van artistieke producties te verzekeren alsook in het belang van het publiek.

Hoofdstuk 4. Een Europees kader voor concurrentie

Samenvatting

De mogelijkheid van grensoverschrijdende televisie via satelliet en/of kabel, doet de noodzaak ontstaan van een Europees reglementair kader. De Europese Gemeenschappen en de Raad van Europa, beiden hetzelfde doel nastrevend – het vrije verkeer van televisie binnen heel Europa – hopen zo'n kader te kunnen creëren. De Commissie van de Europese Gemeenschappen werkt momenteel aan een ontwerprichtlijn en de Raad van Europa aan een voorstel voor een conventie. De wettelijke basis, de rijkwijdte en de strekking van deze twee teksten, op het moment in behandeling op ministerieel niveau, verschilt. Toch is het wenselijk dat de inhoud van de beide teksten zo veel mogelijk overeenkomt.

Wettelijke regelingen bestaan ook met betrekking tot technische zaken (bv. de bepalingen van de *International Telecommunication Union* en de aanbevelingen van de CEPT – *European Conference on Post and Telecommunications Administration*), evenals door vak-organisaties opgestelde normen voor de praktijk (bv. de *European Broadcasting Union*, de *Internationale Kamer van Koophandel* en de *European Advertising Tripartite*).

Deze regels en bepalingen dragen bij, of zullen bijdragen, tot het creëren van een Europees omroep-kader. Toch kan geen van hen op zichzelf een samenhangend en alomvattend Europees omroepbeleid verzekeren, zoals is beschreven in de *Negende Verklaring van de Raad van Gouverneurs van de Europese Culturele Stichting* van 30 mei 1986 (zie Annex 3).

Aanbevelingen

4.1. Aanbevolen wordt om de voorgestelde media-richtlijn van de Commissie van de Europese Gemeenschappen en het voorstel voor een conventie over grensoverschrijdende omroep van de Raad van Europa met elkaar in overeenstemming te brengen. Daarnaast wordt aanbevolen beide instrumenten in werking te laten treden in de mate waarin de maatregelen en bepalingen overeenkomen met de geest van dit Rapport.

4.2. Het principe van quota's voor Europese programma's en eigen productie zou ten minste tijdelijk aanvaard moeten worden. Quota's moeten worden toegepast op alle televisienetten, ongeacht hun wettelijke status of bronnen van inkomsten, ofwel op basis van het totale programma-aanbod ofwel uitsluitend berekend over de totale omvang van drama[1].

4.3. De voorgestelde bepalingen in de ontwerp-richtlijn van de Commissie van de Europese Gemeenschappen die stellen dat de stimulering van audiovisuele productie en distributie uitgebreid zou moeten worden tot de lidstaten van de Raad van Europa en van de *EFTA* – op basis van toekomstige wederzijdse overeenkomsten – dienen door de lidstaten aanvaard te worden.

4.4. De wetgeving met betrekking tot auteursrechten en afgeleide rechten moet herzien en op Europees niveau gecoördineerd worden om het mogelijk te maken voor ontwerpers, schrijvers en uitvoerenden een rechtvaardig deel te ontvangen van de inkomsten die voortvloeien uit de expansie en internationalisering van televisie.

---

1   Dr Peter Schiwy en Sir Ian Trethowan distantiëren zich van elk voorstel tot het opleggen van quota's. Zij zijn van mening dat de aanbevelingen gedaan in de paragrafen 5.1 tot 5.11 voldoende zijn voor de ontwikkeling van een dynamische productie-industrie in Europa.

4.5. Het voorstel in de ontwerp-richtlijn van de Commissie van de Europese Gemeen-schappen om problemen inzake auteursrechten op te lossen door onderhandelingen tussen alle belanghebbende partijen (organisaties voor auteursrechten, producenten, omroepinstellingen en kabelexploitanten) en, in het geval geen overeenkomst moge-lijk is, door arbitrage waarbij de rechthebbenden vertegenwoordigd zijn, dient door de lidstaten aanvaard te worden.

4.6. Het is wenselijk dat .de *European Broadcasting Union* (EBU) grensover-schrijdende omroepinstellingen opneemt in haar kring naast de nationale leden. Als tegenprestatie voor de diensten die de EBU deze nieuwe leden biedt zou de EBU hen moeten verplichten zich te houden aan de gedragsregels van kracht voor de huidige EBU-leden.

Hoofdstuk 5. Een dynamische programma-industrie voor televisie

Samenvatting

De voordelen die de kijker zal hebben als gevolg van de toename in het aantal te ont-vangen netten is afhankelijk van de mogelijkheden voor de omroepinstellingen om een volledig en gevarieerd programma aan te bieden. Hoewel er een aanzienlijke toename heeft plaats gevonden in het aantal programma-uren, stagneert de produc-tie in Europa en daalt deze zelfs in bepaalde gebieden, zoals die van de bioskoopfilm en televisie-drama. Het feit dat men vaak zijn toevlucht zoekt in 'low budget' programma's, herhalingen en geïmporteerde programma's vormt een serieuze be-dreiging voor de kwaliteit van Europese televisie. De invasie van programma's uit landen met een geavanceerde productie-technologie zoals de Verenigde Staten, Japan, Brazilië en Australië, vormt niet alleen een serieus gevaar voor de Europese culturele identiteit, maar ook voor Europa's handelsbalans: het netto tekort op de im-port/export balans van audiovisuele programma's wordt voor 1986 geschat op zo'n 1400 miljoen ecu.

Het ontbreekt in Europa niet aan creatief talent of aan productie capaciteit. De Europese en nationale overheden hebben daarom een belangrijke rol: ze moeten een serie direkte of indirekte maatregelen nemen om de audiovisuele productie-industrie te helpen.

Aanbevelingen

5.1. Steunmaatregelen voor de ontwikkeling van Europese audiovisuele productie vormen een essentiële aanvulling op de toepassing van bepalingen die het vrije verkeer van televisienetten verzekeren.

5.2. Zulke steunmaatregelen zouden niet alleen betrekking moeten hebben op de productie en co-productie van televisie-materiaal, maar ook op de promotie, distributie en uitzending ervan in heel Europa. Hoge prioriteit moet gegeven worden aan het verbeteren van de technische, culturele en economische voorwaarden die van toepassing zijn op het omzetten van de ene taal naar de andere.

5.3. De activiteiten van de Europese Commissie, ondernomen in het kader van het *MEDIA* project en in samenwerking met de betreffende professionele groeperingen op het gebied van productie en uitzendingen van televisie-materiaal en bioskoopfilms, moeten zodanig worden gefinancierd dat zij op bevredigende wijze kunnen worden gerealiseerd en verder ontwikkeld.

5.4. Resolutie No.1 betreffende de stimulering van Europese audiovisuele werken, aangenomen door de Eerste Europese Ministersconferentie over Massamediabeleid in het kader van de Raad van Europa op 9 en 10 december 1986 in Wenen, moet uitgevoerd worden.

5.5. De samenwerking waartoe de Europese Commissie en de Raad van Europa in principe besloten hebben, met als doel de coördinatie van hun activiteiten ter stimulering van de audiovisuele industrie, moet gestalte krijgen.

5.6. De *European Broadcasting Union* (EBU) zou haar initiatieven op het gebied van co-productie en distributie van nieuw audiovisueel materiaal, op het gebied van het verminderen van hindernissen voor meertalige programma's en op het gebied van training van creatieve- en productiestaf verder moeten ontwikkelen.

5.7. Alle Europese landen dienen gebruik te maken van de multilaterale overeenkomsten terzake de co-productie van films en televisie-programma's, gelanceerd onder de naam *EURIMAGES* en de bescherming genietend van de Raad van Europa.

5.8. Bestaande directe steunmaatregelen voor film-productie in de verschillende landen moeten gehandhaafd en uitgebreid worden naar de onafhankelijke productie. Deze regelingen moeten bij voorkeur gefinancierd worden door middel van heffingen op de omzet van de televisie- en filmindustriën zelf en niet door subsidie uit publieke fondsen, die van nature onzeker zijn.

5.9. De volgende fiscale maatregelen moeten, daar waar ze nog niet van kracht zijn, genomen worden:

● de instelling van belastingvoordelen voor investeringen in de audiovisuele programma-industrie;

● het creëren van investeringsfondsen die het kleine investeerders mogelijk maken kapitaal beschikbaar te stellen voor de audiovisuele industrie;

● de harmonisering van wettelijke en fiscale bepalingen met als doel co-productie tussen partners in de Europese landen aan te moedigen;

● de toepassing op de televisie- en filmindustrie van overeengekomen verlaagde BTW-tarieven.

5.10 De financiering van de filmindustrie zou verzekerd moeten worden door een groeiende participatie van televisie-organisaties in filmproductie, alsook door pogingen het bioskoopbezoek op een bevredigend niveau te houden. Tot dit laatste kan een weloverwogen programmering van films op televisie bijdragen.

5.11. Kleinere landen en regio's, waar de audiovisuele industrie het minst ontwikkeld is zouden voorrang moeten krijgen bij steunverlening aan de audiovisuele industrie. Het is eveneens wenselijk dat het Europees Fonds voor Regionale Ontwikkeling in de toekomst speciale aandacht geeft aan steun voor de culturele industrieën in die landen en regio's.

Hoofdstuk 6. Nieuwe Europese televisienetten

Samenvatting

Er bestaan al een aantal televisie-netten in Europa wiens voortbestaan afhankelijk is van een Europees publiek en wiens geografische distributie niet overeenkomt met nationale grenzen. Die netten maken al gebruik van verschillende mogelijkheden geboden door 'fixed satellite services', kabelnetwerken en het toenemend aantal particulieren met eigen ontvangstapparatuur. Hun verplichtingen, manieren van financiering en doelstellingen verschillen. Ze kunnen opgericht zijn door publieke omroepen of commerciële omroepinstellingen, ze kunnen gefinancierd worden door contributies van nationale netten, door subsidies, reclame-gelden, sponsoring of abonnementen. Hun doelstellingen lopen uiteen: van het door heel Europa verspreiden van programma's in een bepaalde taal (bv. **TV5, 3-SAT, Super Channel** en **RAI-Uno**), tot het aanbieden van amusementsprogramma's (bv. **Sky Channel**) en het aanbieden van thematische netten voor een bepaald publiek (bv. **Filmnet, Screen Sport, Arts Channel, MTV Europe** enz.).

In gebieden waar de mogelijkheid bestaat zulke netten en/of netten uit buurlanden te ontvangen bestaat er ook een publiek voor, zij het soms marginaal. Sommige omroepen (bv. **CLT, Canal Plus** en de **Fininvest Group**) geven er de voorkeur aan hun Europese strategie te baseren op het aanbieden van aparte netten voor de verschillende taalgebieden in Europa.

Geen enkele van deze grensoverschrijdende netten biedt een echt Europees programma aan. Problemen met vertaling, culturele verschillen en auteursrechten vormen grote hindernissen voor het oprichten van een echt Europees net. Toch zijn er echte Europese netten nodig en wel om politieke, culturele en economische redenen. Vanuit een politiek standpunt gezien zouden zulke netten het huidige proces van Europese integratie stimuleren. Vanuit een cultureel standpunt gezien zouden ze de uitwisseling van programma's stimuleren, alsook een beter begrip van en goede contacten tussen Europeanen. Vanuit een economisch standpunt gezien zouden ze zorgen voor een goede omzet, met name in het geval van thematische netten, daar Europese netten de toegang zouden hebben tot een potentieel publiek van 125 miljoen huishoudens en 350 miljoen personen.

Aanbevelingen

6.1. Er moeten meertalige Europese televisienetten in het leven worden geroepen, die in het algemeen belang opereren. Deze netten dienen zich in hoofdzaak bezig te houden met kwaliteitsprogramma's, waarbij gebruik wordt gemaakt van de productie mogelijkheden van de verschillende landen, alsook met een Europese nieuwsdienst.

6.2. Een Europese nieuwsdienst dient de vorm te krijgen van een specifiek op nieuws gericht meertalig net. Zo niet, dan zal deze nieuwsdienst geleidelijk moeten worden geïntegreerd in de algemene nationale of Europese televisienetten.

6.3. Zulke Europese omroepen die in het algemeen belang opereren, zouden gefinancierd kunnen worden uit kijk- en luistergelden van de nationale omroepen en door subsidies van regeringen en/of Europese instellingen.

Hoofdstuk 7. Een Europees Televisie Forum

Samenvatting

Het nieuwe Europese televisie-landschap vraagt om nieuwe structuren die rekening houden met de internationalisering en toenemende commercialisering van televisie. Zulke structuren zouden al bestaande structuren als basis kunnen gebruiken, of geheel nieuw opgezet kunnen worden in overeenstemming met de nieuwe eisen.

Een van de meest dringende behoeften is het oprichten van een doelmatige organisatie die zich bezig gaat houden met wat wij de 'derde weg' genoemd hebben, de weg die tot harmonieuze competitie leidt. Hoe meer overeenkomsten er vrijwillig gesloten kunnen worden door de omroepen zelf, des te minder officiële regelgevende organismen er nodig zijn. Gegeven de vele nationale verschillen op dit gebied, lijkt het momenteel niet mogelijk een Europese Televisie Autoriteit in het leven te roepen. De meest uitvoerbare oplossing lijkt dus te zijn een forum op te richten voor debat en uitwisseling tussen de verschillende groepen in Europese televisie — een Europees Televisie Forum.

Aanbevelingen

7.1. De bevindingen in dit rapport hebben de European Television Task Force overtuigd van de noodzaak van een Europese instelling ter stimulering van een evenwichtige en samenhangende ontwikkeling van de Europese televisie.

7.2. Na bestudering van een aantal mogelijke modellen voor zo'n instelling, beveelt de Task Force de oprichting aan van een Europees Televisie Forum.

7.3. Dit Forum zal de vorm moeten hebben van een non-gouvernementele instelling, met een lidmaatschap dat representatief is voor de voornaamste belangen op het gebied van de ontwikkeling van Europese televisie.

7.4. De functie van het Forum zal in eerste instantie bestaan uit het realiseren van de uitvoering van de in dit Rapport gedane aanbevelingen en het initiëren van discussies op maatschappelijk en professioneel niveau aangaande de structuur, inhoud, kwaliteit en invloed van grensoverschrijdende televisie in Europa.

Annex 1
Evidence received by the European Television Task Force

Evidence received in writing is marked W, and that received orally is marked O
Government departments are listed under the name of the country concerned

ANICA, Rome, Italy	*Dr Cianfarani, Carmine, Chairman*	O
ANTENNE 2, Paris, France	*Contamine, Claude, Chairman and Managing Director*	O
ASTRA	*see Société européenne des satellites*	
AUDITEL/UPA, Rome, Italy	*Dr Malgara, Giulio, Chairman, Quaker-Chiari & Forti*	O
Belgische Radio en Televisie (BRT) Brussels, Belgium	*Professor Verhulst, Adriaan, Chairman*	O,W
	Goossens, Cas, Managing Director	O
British Broadcasting Corporation (BBC) London, United Kingdom	*Howell, James, Director of Corporate Affairs*	O
	Hart, Alan, Controller of International Relations	O,W
	Hodgson, Paul, Head of International Relations	O
	Jennings, Anthony, Legal Adviser	O
Bundesverband Kabel und Satellit e.v. (BKS TV), Bonn, FRG	*Grosse Peclum, Marie-Louise, Vice-chairman*	O
Bureau européen des unions de consommateurs (BEUC), Brussels, Belgium	*Schmitz, Robert, Legal Adviser*	W
Cable Authority, London, United Kingdom	*Davey, John, Director General*	O,W

Christlich Demokratische Union/Christlich Soziale Union Deutschlands (CDU/CSU), Bonn, FRG	*Dr Weirich, M.d.B. CDU/CSU, Parliamentary spokesman (media policy), Member of Board of Directors, ZDF*	O
Christen Democratisch Appel (CDA), The Hague, Netherlands	*Dr Klop, C J, Vice Director of the Scientific Institute of CDA*	O,W
CLT/RTL-PLUS, Luxemburg	*Dr. Neuen, Jacques, General Secretary*	O
Confédération des organisations familiales de la Communauté européenne (COFACE), Brussels, Belgium	*Lay, William, Director*	W
Commission of the European Communities, Brussels, Belgium:		
Directorate General III (Internal Market and Industrial Affairs)	*Lord Cockfield, Vice President of the Commission, Dr Schwartz, Ivo, Director Dr Brühann, Ulf, Principal Administrator*	O O,W O,
Directorate General IV (Competition)	*Sutherland, Peter D, Commissioner Overbury, Henry Colin, Director*	W O
Directorate General X (Information, Communication and Culture)	*Ripa di Meana, Carlo, Commissioner Maggiore, Mariano, Head of Division for Cultural activities and audiovisual policy*	O,W O
Commission nationale de la communication et des libertés (CNCL), Paris, France	*de Broglie, Gabriel, President*	O
Conseil supérieur de l'audiovisuel, communauté française, Brussels, Belgium,	*Brassine, J, President*	W
Council of Protestant Churches in Germany, Frankfurt, FRG	*Hessler, Hans-Wolfgang, Television Commissioner*	W

Danmarks Radio (DR), Soeborg, Denmark	*Antonson, Henrik, Acting Chairman NORDVISION, Director of Television Programmes*	**O,W**
	Grausen, Bruno, Head of Legal Department	O
Denmark: Ministry of Culture, Copenhagen, Denmark	*Rasmussen, Harder J, Deputy Secretary*	O
	Nielsen, Niels-Jorgen, Head of Media Department	O
	Norup-Nielsen, J, Head of Copyright Department	O
	Petersen, Vibekeg, Expert in the Media Department	O
Ente Autonomo Gestione Cinema, Rome, Italy	*Dr Grippo, Ivo, Chairman*	O
European Association of Advertising Agencies (EAAA) & European Advertising Tripartite (EAT), Brussels, Belgium	*De Win, Paul, Chairman EAT Satellite Committee*	O
	Tempest, Alastair, Secretary EAT, EAAA	W
European Broadcasting Union (EBU), Geneva, Switzerland	*Schurf, Albert, President*	O
	Vilcek, Miro, Head of television programme division	W
European Committee of Trade Unions in Arts, Mass Media and Entertainment, Brussels, Belgium	*Ratterton, Pierre*	O
	Roefs, Jean-Louis	O
European Federation of Audiovisual Filmmakers (FERA), Brussels, Belgium	*Correa, João, General Secretary*	W
European Graphical Federation, Brussels, Belgium	*Griffith, David,Vice President*	O
	Kaufmann, A, General Secretary	O

European Parliament, Luxemburg:

Directorate General III	*Barzanti, Roberto, MEP*	O
(Information and Public	*Collowald, Paul, Director General*	O
Relations)		
Directorate General IV	*Lensen, Anton*	W
(Research)		
European Telecommunications	*Caruso, A, General Manager*	W
Satellite Organization		
(EUTELSAT), Paris, France		
European Trade Union	*Hinterscheid, Mathias, General*	W
Confederation (ETUC), Brussels,	*Secretary*	
Belgium	*Rath, Fritz, Political Secretary*	O
	Bergans, Wim, Press and Information	O
	Officer	
	Roefs, Jean-Louis	O
Fédération internationale des	*Gregoire, Gilbert, Deputy Director*	W
associations de distributeurs de		
films (FIAD), Paris, France		
FERA	*see European Federation of*	
	Audiovisual Filmmakers	
FININVEST, Milan, Italy	*Berlusconi, Silvio, Chairman*	O,W
Finland :		
Ministry of Education	*Numminen, Jaakko, Secretary General,*	W
	Chairman of the National Committee	
	on Media Culture	
	Haulat, Kristina, Secretary	W
France :		
Ministry of Communication,	*Santini, André, Secretary of State for*	O
Paris, France	*Communication*	O
	Mongrand, Jean-Pierre, Technical	
	Adviser	
Senat, Commission des	*Cluzel, Jean, Special Rapporteur*	W
Finances, Paris, France		

CNCL	*see Commission nationale de la communication et des libertés*	
Commission d'orientation du câble	*Luliez, Michel*	0
Freie Demokratische Partei Deutschlands (FDP) Media Commission, Bonn, FRG	*Eggers, Ernst, Secretary of State, Ministry of Economics and Transport, Rhineland-Palatinate*	O
Gallaher Tobacco (UK) Ltd Surrey, United Kingdom	*Boxall, R R, Director*	W
Gesellschaft für musikalische Auffürungs- und mechanische Vervielfältigungsrechte / Spitzenverband Deutsche Musik (GEMA/SPIDEM), Bonn, FRG	*Prof Dr Schulze, Erich, President* *Dr Steinschulte, Gabriel M.* *General Secretary*	O O
Germany (Federal Republic):		
Auswärtiges Amt, Bonn, FRG	*Dr Witte, Bartold C,* *Ministerial -Direktor,* *Sommer, Klaus-Dieter, Vortragender* *Legationsrat*	O O
Innenministerium, Bonn, FRG	*Merk, Hans-Günther, Head of Department of Sports and Media* *Dr Wilhelm, Bernhard, Referatsleiter* *Höfling, Heribert, Ministerialrat*	O O O
Granada Television, Manchester, United Kingdom	*Plowright, David, Chairman*	W
Groupe Bruxelles Lambert S A Brussels, Belgium	*de Goldschmidt, Frédéric, Attaché de Direction*	O

Independent Broadcasting Authority (IBA), London, United Kingdom	*Lord Thomson of Monifieth, Chairman*	O
	Whitney, John, Director General	O
	Glencross, David,	O
	Director of Television	O
	Blyth, Kenneth,	
	Chief Assistant (Director General)	O
	Dr Forrest, John,	
	Director of Engineering	O
	Willis, Frank, Controller of Advertising	
Independent Television Association Ltd, London, United Kingdom	*Shaw, David, General Secretary*	W
	Barton, Trevor,	W
	Regional Companies Secretary	
International Federation of Journalists, Brussels, Belgium	*White, Aidan, General Secretary*	O,W
International Federation of Phonogram and Videogram Producers, London, United Kingdom	*Orf, Ewald, Legal Adviser*	W
Italy:		
Ministry of Posts and Telecommunications, Rome, Italy	*Mammi, Oscar, Minister*	O
KRO	*see Stichting Katholieke Radio Omroep*	
LA SEPT, Paris, France	*Anthonioz, Michel, Assistant Director General of programmes*	O
Logica Consultancy Ltd, London, United Kingdom	*D'Abreu, Anthony, Senior Consultant*	W
M 6, Paris, France	*Drucker, Jean, Director General*	O
Mirror Group Newspapers, London, United Kingdom	*Jay, Peter, Chief of Staff*	W
Nederlands Omroepproduktie Bedrijf (NOB), Hilversum, Netherlands	*Hindriks, Klaas Jan, Director International Relations*	O

Nederlandse Omroep Stichting	*van den Heuvel, A, Vice President*	O
(NOS), Hilversum, Netherlands	*van der Haak, C P M, Head of*	O
	Combined Programme Services	
	Hendriksen, Paul, Head International	O
	Affairs Department	
Netherlands		
Ministry of Welfare, Health and	*Kramer, H Y, Head Directorate*	W
Cultural Affairs, The Hague	*Radio, Television and Press*	
	Overste, A M, Head Section General	O
	Policy Development of Directorate	
	Radio, Television & Press	
	Reynders, A D, Section General	O
	Policy Development of Directorate	
	Radio, Television & Press	
Norsk Rikskringkasting (NRK),	*Gjerde, Bjartmar, Director General*	O
Oslo, Norway	*Smeland, Sverre, Chief Secretary*	O
Norway:		
Ministry of Culture and	*Soenneland, Helge, Deputy Director*	O
Science, Oslo	*General*	
	Kristiansen, Roy, Assistant Deputy	O
	Director General	
ODEON TV, Rome, Italy	*di Tondo, Marcello , Chairman*	O
Oesterreichischer Rundfunk	*Zeiler, Gerhard, Secretary General*	W
(ORF) Vienna, Austria		
Oy Yleidsradio Ab, Helsinki,	*Soramaki, Martti, Head of Media*	W
Finland	*Development Group*	
Pierson, Heldring & Pierson N.V.	*De Haas, Bart F A,*	O
Amsterdam, Netherlands	*Directeur Trustzaken*	
Portugal:	*dos Santos, Conto, Assistant Minister*	O
Ministry of Communication	*to the Prime Minister*	
	Suares, Albino, Secretary of State for	
	Social Communication	
Radio Telefís Eireann (RTE),	*Finn, Vincent, Director General*	O
Dublin, Ireland		

Radio télévision belge de la communauté française (RTBF) Brussels, Belgium	*Hallet, Jean, Chairman* *Stéphane, Robert,* *Director General*	O O
Radio Televisione España (RTVE), Madrid, Spain	*Martin, Jesus, Director*	O
Radiotelevisao Portuguesa EP (RTP), Lisbon, Portugal	*Dr Coelho Ribeiro, José Manuel, Chairman*	O
RAI Radiotelevisione Italiana	*Manca, Enrico, Chairman* *Dr Agnes, Biagio, Director General*	O O
Sanoma Corporation Helsinki, Finland	*Anderzen, Matti, Executive Vice President*	W
Satellite Television plc (Sky Channel), London, England	*Cruthers, Sir James, Chairman* *Cox, Patrick, Chief Executive and Deputy Chairman* *Styles, Jim, Managing Director*	O,W O O
Sozialdemokratische Partei Deutschlands (SDP), Bonn, FRG	*Dr Glotz, Peter, MP,* *Media policy Commissioner*	O
Societe européenne des satellites (SES), Luxemburg	*Dr Meyrat, Pierre, Managing Director* *Bicknell, Marcus, Marketing Director*	O W
Spain : **Ministry of Culture, Madrid**	*Solana, Javier, Minister of Culture*	O
Stichting Katholieke Radio Omroep (KRO), Hilversum, Netherlands	*Dr Schoonhoven, Richard, Director*	O
Super Channel, London, United Kindom	*Hooper, Richard, Managing Director*	O
	Levison, Charles, Managing Director of Virgin Broadcasting	O
Sveriges Radio (SR), Stockholm, Sweden	*Wallquist, Oerjan, Director General*	O

Sweden:

Ministry of Education and Cultural Affairs	*Göransson, Bengt, Minister of Culture*	O,W
	Blanck, Britt-Marie, *Deputy Assistant Under-Secretary*	O
	Maren, Lars, *Deputy Assistant Under-Secretary*	O
Télédiffusion de France, Paris, France	*Georgy, Jean, Assistant Director for* *Spatial Affairs*	O
Télévision française 1 (TF1), Paris, France	*Le Lay, P, Vice President*	O
TV5, Paris, France	*Celerier, Jean-Jacques,* *Director General*	W
UFA Film- und Fernseh GmbH, Hamburg, FRG	*Schiphorst, Bernd, Managing Director*	W
	Faisst, Thomas, Director *International Development*	W
United Kingdom Home Office, London	*Renton, Timothy, MP,* *Minister of State*	O,W
	Thomas, Quentin, Under Secretary, *Broadcasting Department*	O,W
	Wright, Paul, Assistant Secretary *International Division,* *Broadcasting Department*	O,W
VARA Omroepvereniging, Hilversum, Netherlands	*Dr van Wijk, H, General Manager*	W
VERONICA / Veronica Omroep Organisatie (VOO), Hilversum, Netherlands	*Meyers, Constant, Producer*	O
Volunteer Centre, Herts, UK	*Stubbings, Peter, Deputy Director*	W
Wallonie Bruxelles Images, Brussels, Belgium	*Barnet, Rudi*	W
ZDF/3-SAT	*Dr Konrad, Walter, Co-ordinator*	O
Zweites Deutsches Fernsehen (ZDF), Mainz-Lerchenberg, FRG	*Professor Stolte, Dieter, Director* *General*	W

Annex 2
Glossary

This Glossary has been compiled to assist readers of the Report to understand the technical terms and abbreviations.

Above-the-line: In *advertising*, the cost of placing advertisements in media where the advertiser pays for the airtime or space (TV, print, radio, billboards, cinema); all other promotional publicity expenditures are "**below-the-line**" (consumer promotions, trade deals, price cuts, sales brochures, PR, etc.).
In *television production*, creative costs (writers, directors, producers, and main cast); as opposed to technical and promotional expenses.

Add-on services: Television services, such as pay-TV or VCR (video cassette recorders) which are bought by some homes to give programme choices additional to the "mainstream" broadcast channels available in all TV homes in the area and which people watch most of the time.

Addressability: Technical interaction between the transmitting station (or cable head-end) and each individual receiving household, which allows measurement of viewing of specific programmes or channels.

Affiliates: TV stations which by contract receive most of their broadcast material from a particular network but are not owned by that network.

Aspect ratio: The ratio of a screen's width to its height, currently 4:3 for television. Cinema and HDTV have an aspect ratio of about 5:3.

ASTRA: A medium power satellite due to be launched at the end of 1988 and belonging to the Société européenne des Satellites, which will rent out its 16 channels to programme providers.

Audience duplication, Audience overlap: The viewers which two broadcasters have in common.

181

Audience inheritance, lead-in effect: The tendency for a programme to have extra audience overlap with the adjacent programmes on the same channel.

Audience ratings, ratings: The percentage of a particular population watching a television programme at a specific time. Usually measures the people who are in the room with the set switched on. "Household ratings" or "set ratings" refer to the percentage of households with a set on tuned to the programme.

Cable: A wired distribution system delivering television, and possibly other services, direct to the homes of subscribers.

Cable headend: The point of origination of individual cable systems, from which the various services offered are sent to the subscribers

Camcorder: Short for camera/recorder, i.e. a light, portable unit combining the functions of video camera and recorder.

CATV: Community Antenna Television. Homes in a united area, which suffer from poor over-air reception, are cabled to a large, shared aerial.

Channel: Strictly speaking the assigned band of frequencies on which an individual programme service is broadcast. In practice, the term has come to be used to identify the sequence of programmes offered by a single programme provider

Commercial Break: When programme broadcasts are interrupted to transmit one or more paid-for advertisements.

Complementary programming: When one TV station transmits a very different type of programme from another at a given time, thus giving viewers a wider choice of programme types at that time.

Co-productions: Programmes whose production costs are shared by two or more broadcasting organisations, usually in different countries.

Diary methods: People recording their television-viewing activities, usually quarter-hour by quarter-hour in a pre-structured 7-day "diary".Also see **audience ratings**

DBS: Direct Broadcasting Satellite. Satellites with high power (up to 200 Watt) transponders, intended for direct public reception and broadcasting in the 12-14GHz band. At the time of writing, there are no working DBS satellites in Europe.

Downlink: Reception of signals from a satellite, also called **Download.**

EBU: The European Broadcasting Union, the association of national public-service broadcasters in the ITU Western European Broadcasting area.

Encoded programmes: Programmes sent in scrambled form, capable of being unscrambled with the use of a de-coder supplied against payment by the programme provider.

Encryption: See encoded programmes

First-run: The first showing of a programme or series.

FSS: Fixed Service Satellite. Low-power satellites transmitting in the 10-12 GHz band, intended for reception by specified organisations such as telecommunications systems, cable operators, broadcasting stations receiving programme feeds etc. FSS transmissions are in theory not available for public reception (see **DBS**).

HDTV: High Definition Television. Television recording and transmission systems containing more picture information than the systems currently in use, which are either:
525 lines/60Hz used in North America and Japan
625 lines/50Hz used elsewhere in the world.
Proposed standards for HDTV include the use of more lines to make up the picture, higher frequency of repetition of the frames and a different **aspect ratio** (q.v.).

Independents ("indies"): In the USA, local stations that function independently of the networks. Often the stations are linked in chains across several cities, forming co-operative "mini-networks", or are grouped under the same ownership. The term **independents** is also used to describe television production companies which are not owned by a broadcasting organisation or major film studio.

In-house: Television programmes which are produced by the broadcasting organisation itself instead of being bought from independent producers or other broadcasters.

Interactive (or "two-way") cable: Cables with capacity to transmit signals both ways between cable subscribers and the head-end, so that viewers can send or request information via the system instead of, say, by telephone.

ITU: The International Telecommunication Union. An international body in which governments are represented by officials of their broadcasting frequency regulatory agencies. ITU lays down the regulatory framework for the use of the radio frequency spectrum

LPTV: Low Power Television, a type of local broadcast station with a limit on its licensed power output, to avoid interference with other stations' signals.

MAC: Multiplexed Analogue Components. A system of digital encoding and transmission of television signals, intially proposed for use by satellite transponders. There are several variants of the system, generically described as the MAC Packet family of systems. Programmes broadcast under any of the MAC standards cannot be displayed by receivers not specifically equipped to show them.

MMDS: Microwave Multipoint Distribution System. The transmission of up to 30 channels of television over a radius of some 6 km from the point of broadcast, for direct reception in the home. The frequencies used are in the same band as those used for DBS (q.v.)

Network: A number of television stations linked, either directly or in simultaneous broadcast, to show a common programme.

NTSC: National Television Standards Committee. The system of colour television used in North America and Japan. Signals transmitted using the NTSC system cannot be displayed by PAL or SECAM receivers.

OIRT: Organisation international de la radiodiffusion et de la télévision. The association grouping national broadcasting services in the member states of Comecon.

PAL: Phase Alternating Line. A system of colour television widely used in Western Europe (excepting France), Latin America, Asia and the non-French-speaking territories of the Pacific. There are three variants: PAL-B, used in the United Kingdom and Ireland, and PAL-G and PAL-I, used elsewhere.Receivers capable of recieving PAL-B signals cannot receive the sound channel of PAL-G and PAL-I without internal adjustment.

PAL-625: This refers to television signals transmitted at 625-lines/50Hz using the PAL colour television system.

Pay-per-view: The process of charging for television services according to individual programmes accepted by the viewer, rather than by **subscription** (q.v.) to the channel as a whole.

Pay-TV: Any system in which viewers pay on an individual household basis for the right to watch a particular channel.

Peak viewing: Times when the largest number of people tend to be viewing television; generally between 1900 and 2200 hours, but it may differ from one country to another. (See also **prime time**)

People-meters: Electronic push-button devices to record the presence of individual viewers when measuring audience ratings. Always employed on "panel" surveys; often used to replace diary methods.

Prime time: Those hours when the television ratings are highest. Used with very specific time limits, which differ from one country to another, in connection with the costs of air-time for commercials. (and see **Peak Viewing**)

PTT: Posts, telephones and telegraphs- a generic term used to describe the authorities, public or private, providing these services in various countries. There is an increasing tendency in Europe and elsewhere to separate the activities of the telephone and electronic communications services (telecoms) from the letter-carrying services of the post.

Public Service Broadcasting: Broadcasting services whose primary aim is the provision of a full service of television to the viewing public, according to the terms of a charter, mandate or other document setting out the responsibilities and obligations of the service. Such services may be financed by licence fee, advertising revenue or a combination of both.

Ratings war: A form of competition between television channels (stations, networks, etc.) in which each strives at each point in time for the largest possible audience (within the restrictions of its programming budgets).

Residuals: Contractual payments to actors, writers etc — over and above an initial fee — when a programme is shown for a second time or in another market. Also known as repeat fees.

Royalty: Contractual payments to actors, writers etc made at intervals and based on a proportion of sales or revenues to date (rather than a one-off fee).

Scrambled programmes: See encoded programmes.

SECAM: Séquentiel couleur à mémoire. A system of colour television used in France and the member states of OIRT. SECAM signals cannot be correctly displayed on **PAL** (q.v.) receivers.

Segmentation: Any marked tendency for a separately identifiable subgroup of the population to have similar tastes or behaviour (e.g. viewing a particular television programme, buying a particular brand or product), especially when they can also be identified in some other way as reachable targets for advertising purposes (e.g. young mothers, owners of hi-fi equipment, etc.).

Serials: Continuing programmes where individual episodes have a self-contained plot, but use more or less the same cast of main characters.

Series: Narrative programmes which have a continuing storyline over a sequence of episodes and tell the story to its conclusion.

Smart Card: A plastic card which contains a printed electronic circuit which is programmed (smart) to allow the user to unscramble transmitted signals and to note how much it has been used. It is a development of the laser-read cards used in some public telephones.

SMATV: Satellite Master Antenna Television, a private multichannel cable system for a hotel or apartment block.

Soap opera: A type of programme series with an ongoing melodramatic plot. So-named because such drama serials on US radio were originally sponsored by a soap manufacturer. Examples are *East Enders, Coronation Street, Schwartzwaldklinik, Châteauvallon, Dallas* and *Dynasty.* Also see **telenovela**.

Subscription television: A service of television broadcast over the air, by satellite or by cable and available only to viewers who have paid a fee to receive the service. Most subscription services are **encoded**, q.v.

Thematic channel; A television service concentrating for the most part on one specific area of programming. Examples include channels devoted entirely to films, weather reports, sports, popular music etc.

Syndication: Where a television series is sold (syndicated) to different broadcasting organisations in different parts of the same country (especially in the US). Programmes are usually syndicated after a successful network run, but there is now also a growing trade in "first-run syndication".

Telenovela: A melodramatic series, usually broadcast each day, in which a story is told to its conclusion (so differing from **soap operas**,(q.v.) which may run indefinitely. Telenovelas originated in Brazil, but have found much popularity with European audiences. The average telenovela runs for some 156 episodes.

Teletext: Transmission of text as part of the picture information in the signal broadcast by a television service. The text can only be seen by the viewer if a teletext decoder is used.

Time-shift: Using a VCR to record a programme off-air for playback at a later (preferred) time.

Trailer: An announcement or promotion about a programme or its next episode, transmitted by the broadcaster (not a "paid-for" advertisement).

Transponder: Part of a satellite. The transponder receives signals sent from the ground station and re-transmits them on a different frequency for reception within the coverage area of the satellite.

TVRO: Television Receive Only, a generic term used to describe the equipment used in the home to receive and view programmes from satellites.

Uplink: The transmission of signals from a ground station to a satellite.

VCR: Video Cassette Recorder: A machine to record and replay television pictures.

187

Annex 3
9th Declaration of the Board of Governors of the European Cultural Foundation adopted on May 30th 1986

Towards A Coherent Media Policy In Europe

The Board of Governors of the European Cultural Foundation

- recognising the need to guarantee the free flow of information across frontiers;

- recognising the need to give expression to the growing interdependence of European countries and the interdependence in the field of mass communications of these countries;

- noting that problems arising from the development of satellite systems covering several European countries cannot be solved by national protectionism but rather by harmonious cooperation at a European level;

- noting that the multiplication of television programmes broadcast by cable and satellite is not necessarily extending the quality of programmes available, but is running the risk of a decline in cultural content;

- bearing in mind the significance of radio and television as a means of communication at local and regional levels;

- noting the technological changes affecting the structure and organisation of the print media in all European countries;

- noting the growing dependence of the mass media on advertising revenue;

calls on governments, European institutions and local and regional authorities to take the following measures to promote the role of the media in the maintenance and development of European culture:

1. The strengthening of the European audiovisual industry:

(a) by providing tax incentives to investment in original production;

(b) by establishing funds for original creation on a regional, national and European level;

(c) by encouraging and facilitating co-production and co-financing by European partners;

(d) by the exchange of programmes and reinforcing the export of European programmes throughout the world.

(e) by encouraging private patronage.

2. The commitment, faced with the growing commercialisation in the audiovisual sector, to:

(a) guarantee adequate financial means to the public service broadcasting organisations, so enabling them to fulfil the full range of their functions, including education, culture and programmes serving minority groups;

(b) encourage television and radio stations - both private and public - to contribute directly or indirectly to the support of original production;

(c) encourage public and private organisations to include in their services appropriate proportion of programmes originating outside the established broadcasting organisations;

(d) encourage public and private organisations to give positive support to European works of quality;

(e) promote education in the discriminating use of the media.

3. To support:

(a) the protection of the diversity of information sources, as well as the diversity of languages, at the national and the European levels;

(b) the guarantee of editorial independence in the private and public press and broadcasting organisations;

(c) the role of local radio stations as instruments of service to the community, and of participation by the citizens;

(d) the harmonisation of European legislation on copyright and related rights;

(e) the definition of common criteria governing advertising and sponsorship in the media.

To this end, the Board of Governors of the European Cultural Foundation:

● taking account of its declaration of 29 April 1978 on "television and the free circulation of ideas";

● taking account of its eighth declaration of 7 June 1985 and of the intention expressed therein to promote communications on the environment, especially through television and other media;

● bearing in mind the designation of the year 1988 as the European year of film and television;

will reinforce the capability of its network of institutions and centres and in particular of the European Institute for the Media to:

● undertake research aimed at achieving the objectives set out in this Declaration;

● promote consultation about the media aims in this Declaration among the professional and the consumer interests in the press, radio and television in private and public sector organisations;

- develop, on the basis of such research and consultation, practical proposals for a coherent media policy in Europe;

- promote training courses and the exchange of staff responsible for programme production;

- award a European prize for work by radio and television producers at local and regional levels.

Amsterdam, May 30th 1986

Publications of the European Institute for the Media

Europe 2000: What kind of television? is the eleventh in the series of *Media Monographs*, published by the European Institute for the Media.Other titles available in the series are:-

Access to Political Broadcasting in the European Community
Geoffrey Roberts, 1984. English : ISBN 0 7190 1481 6.
French: ISBN 07190 1482 4 £7.50

Advertising, Cable and Satellite: the Elements of the European Debate
Eliane Couprie, 1984. English & French editions: £8.00

European Media Aid to the Third World
John Roper & Cornelia Goeyvaerts, 1986. English : ISBN 0 948195 08 8
French : ISBN 0 948195 01 1 £14.50

Television in Europe: Quality and Values in a Time of Change *Anthony Pragnell*,
1985. English : ISBN 0 948195 00 2. French : ISBN: 0 948195 01 0 £20.00

Mass Communications in Western Europe: An Annotated Bibliography
edited by *George Wedell, Georg-Michael Luyken* and *Rosemary Leonard*,
1985. Multilingual ISBN: 0 948195 04 5 £25.00

Local Radio and Regional Development in Europe
Philip Crookes and *Patrick Vittet-Philippe*, 1986.
English: ISBN 0 948195 07 X £20.00

Media in Competition: the Future of Print and Electronic Media in 22 Countries
George Wedell & Georg-Michael Luyken, 1986.
English : ISBN 3 926074 00 0 £20.00

Towards a European Common Market for Television: Contribution to the Debate, *Eliane Couprie* and *André Lange* English: ISBN 0 948195 12 6
French:ISBN 0 948195 11 8 £25

Freedom of Communication under the Law: Case Studies in six countries
Eliane Couprie & Henry Olssson. English: ISBN 0 948195 14 2.
French: ISBN 0 948195 13 4 £25

The Future of the European Audiovisual Industry,
André Lange, English and French editions (forthcoming)

Overcoming Language Barriers in Television:
Dubbing and Sub-titling for the European audience,
English and French editions (forthcoming)

The *Media Monographs* are distributed by:
Haigh & Hochland Ltd.,
International University Booksellers,
Manchester, M13 9QA England, Telephone (+ 44 61) 272 4156

The European Institute for the Media also publishes the quarterly
European Media Bulletin, in English and French,
available for £15 for one year, or £25 for two years, from:
Subscriptions Department (M11)
The European Institute for the Media,
The University,
Manchester,
M13 9PL-GB
Telephone (+ 44 61) 273 2754 Telex 94011070 EURO G